GEORGE J. "RHINO" THOMPSON
HAMMETT'S MORAL VISION

Vince Emery: "If you haven't read Thompson, you don't know Hammett."

William F. Nolan: "Incredibly well done, beautifully researched, and displaying tremendous insight into what made Hammett tick as a writer. . . . [Thompson's] vision is timeless."

Julian Symons: "One of the most intelligent critics of Hammett's work."

Hammett's Moral Vision is the single most influential full-length investigation of Dashiell Hammett's novels, even though it has never been available in book form—until now.

Serialized in seven issues of *The Armchair Detective* magazine, *Hammett's Moral Vision* has affected almost all subsequent analyses of Hammett's work. But most people could read it only by digging up all seven tough-to-find issues of *The Armchair Detective*, and only for collector's prices of more than $100 per set.

Now *Hammett's Moral Vision* is available as an affordable book. It updates and expands George J. "Rhino" Thompson's analysis of *Red Harvest, The Dain Curse, The Maltese Falcon, The Glass Key,* and *The Thin Man,* and adds a new introduction by Edgar Award-winning author William F. Nolan.

THE ACE
PERFORMER
COLLECTION

"Hammett was the ace performer.
. . . He did over and over again what only
the best writers ever do at all."

—Raymond Chandler

THE ACE PERFORMER COLLECTION
is a series of books
by and about Dashiell Hammett:

VOLUME 1:
Lost Stories
by Dashiell Hammett

VOLUME 2:
Discovering The Maltese Falcon and Sam Spade
edited by Richard Layman

VOLUME 3:
Hammett's Moral Vision
by George J. "Rhino" Thompson

FORTHCOMING:

The Crime Wave: Collected Nonfiction
by Dashiell Hammett

The Films of Dashiell Hammett
by Vince Emery

ADDITIONAL VOLUMES
TO BE ANNOUNCED

HAMMETT'S

Vince Emery

PRODUCTIONS ®

SAN FRANCISCO

The most influential
full-length investigation
of Dashiell Hammett's novels
Red Harvest, The Dain Curse,
The Maltese Falcon, The Glass Key,
and The Thin Man

MORAL VISION

GEORGE J. "RHINO" THOMPSON

Introduction by Edgar Award winner William F. Nolan
Preface by Vince Emery

Hammett's Moral Vision
by George J. "Rhino" Thompson
Introduction by William F. Nolan
Preface by Vince Emery

Published by Vince Emery Productions
P.O. Box 460279
San Francisco, California 94146 USA

www.emerybooks.com

**Vince Emery Productions produces books and videos
by and about established writers
to give readers a deeper, closer connection
with their favorite authors.**

Book design and composition by Desktop Miracles
Del LeMond, Designer
Thanks to Keith J. Sinclair for rapid typing.
Printed and bound in the United States of America.

The paper used in this book complies with the standard for the Permanence of Paper for Publications and Documents for Libraries and Archives issued by the National Information Standards Organization [ANSI/NISO Z39.48 – 1992 (R1997)] and the ISO standard Information and Documentation – Paper for Documents – Requirements for Permanence (ISO 9706: 1994).

FIRST HARDCOVER EDITION
First printing
January 2007

9 8 7 6 5 4 3 2 1

ISBN-10: 0–9725898–3-X
ISBN-13: 978-0-97-258983-3

Dedicated to my planned,
"late-in-life" son,
Tommy Rhyno Thompson,
who is the "wind beneath my wings"
and to his beautiful mom,
my wife, Pam,
who makes life so worth living!

—Doc Thompson

CONT

E N T S

PREFACE

If You Haven't Read Thompson

BY VINCE EMERY

I F YOU HAVEN'T READ Thompson, you don't know Hammett. [1]
How can I say that? Because George J. "Rhino" Thompson illuminates Hammett's works. Reading Thompson helps
you ask the right questions, then helps you answer them.

You might disagree with some of his thought-provoking
conclusions. I do myself.

Even so, you can't understand Hammett's work without
awareness of the issues that Thompson raises. You need clues
from Hammett's own words, and Thompson shows you where
to find them. He points out relevant comments from other
critics' works.

He adds observations of his own, and they are sometimes surprising, often revealing, always intelligent. British biographer and mystery author Julian Symons called Thompson "one of the most intelligent critics of Hammett's work."[1]

Hammett's Moral Vision is the single most influential full-length investigation of Dashiell Hammett's novels: *Red Harvest, The Dain Curse, The Maltese Falcon, The Glass Key,* and *The Thin Man.* Thompson's work has achieved legendary status among Hammettologists, even though only a few dedicated scholars have ever seen it.

How did it become so influential? Thompson originally wrote "The Problem of Moral Vision in Dashiell Hammett's Detective Novels" for his doctoral dissertation at the University of Connecticut at Storrs back in 1972. It was serialized in seven issues of *The Armchair Detective* magazine from 1973 to 1975.

In his book *The Critical Response to Dashiell Hammett,* Christopher Metress declares, "Thompson's study was the first extensive critical analysis of Hammett's fiction." Metress also points out that Thompson was the first to evaluate other critics and what they have said about Hammett's fiction.[2]

Not only is he a pioneer, but out of hundreds of commentators on Hammett's writing, Thompson remains one of the most insightful. He has influenced almost all subsequent analyses of Hammett's novels.

The most surprising fact about Thompson's work is that it has never been available in book form. People could read Thompson only by digging up all seven tough-to-find issues of *The Armchair Detective,* and only for collector's prices. (To collect my set, I searched for nearly a year and paid $178.)

Now *Hammett's Moral Vision* is available as an affordable book, revised and updated throughout, with an index and a new introduction by William F. Nolan, the Edgar Award winning author of *Hammett: A Life at the Edge* and *Logan's Run.*

[2]

In addition, a new chapter by Thompson explains how reading Hammett transformed his life and led him to change careers from English teacher to law enforcement officer.

If you want a deep understanding of Hammett's novels, the very different meanings they have for different readers, and why Hammett changes peoples' lives, you could do worse than starting here.

And you'll pay less than I did.

George J. Thompson's "The Problem of Moral Vision in Dashiell Hammett's Detective Novels" was serialized in The Armchair Detective *beginning with this May 1973 issue, volume 6: number 3. It is now a rare collectible.*

INTRODUCTION

In Hammett Country

BY WILLIAM F. NOLAN

GEORGE THOMPSON AND I are fellow pioneers in Dashiell
Hammett country. He wrote the first full-length critical
study on Hammett, and I wrote the first full-length *book* on
Hammett. Therefore, it is wholly appropriate for me to intro-
duce you to Thompson's pioneering work, presented here in
its initial appearance between covers. Before I do, however, I'd
like you to take a trip with me, back four decades, to April of
1964...

I was in my mid-thirties then, living in Los Angeles, and I'd
been writing full-time for eight years. A friend asked if I'd ever
read anything by Dashiell Hammett.

In June of 1968—after eleven months of research and writing—my 41,000-word manuscript was complete: a combination of biography and literary criticism, with the biographical side predominant.

I contacted author Kenneth Millar ("Ross Macdonald"), who I knew had an abiding interest in Hammett. From his home in Santa Barbara, Millar not only guided me through the final revision of the manuscript, but provided a blurb for the dust jacket. Millar approved a small press house of quality in Santa Barbara, McNally & Loftin, and I signed with them to publish my book in hardcover. The miniscule advance of $200.00 against royalties did not begin to cover my research expenses, but I didn't complain. I'd written the book for personal satisfaction, not for profit.

Dashiell Hammett: A Casebook was published in May of 1969, with an introduction by Philip Durham and 127 pages of text; it was backed by a fifty-page checklist bibliography which listed everything I'd been able to find written by or about Hammett.[1] Considering that my book originated from a small, unknown press in Santa Barbara, California, and was limited to a printing of just one thousand copies, it received extremely wide review coverage. Apparently, critics had been eagerly awaiting a substantial work on Hammett.

I had never expected such praise for my modest undertaking as I knew my book was far from definitive and had said so in my preface. No one commented on its lack of photographs or chapter notes.[2]

Despite the fact that this first book on Hammett is now outdated, having been superseded by many others of more substance (including several key books by Hammett authority Richard Layman), the bibliography still retains solid research value, which is gratifying.

Since the 1960s, Hammett has exerted a profound and lasting influence on my work. From him, I learned to write leaner prose, tougher dialogue, and to adopt a harder-edged tone.

In 1971 I began a series of wild science fiction/detective parody thrillers (*Space for Hire, Look Out for Space, 3 for Space*) directly inspired by Sam Spade. My super-tough private eye, who works out of a seedy office on Mars, was shamelessly named Sam Space. Great fun, and I'll wager Dash would have been amused.

In 1983, as a follow-up to *Casebook*, my *Hammett: A Life at the Edge*—which I consider to be an interim biography—was published. (I will have much more to say about Dashiell Hammett in my forthcoming biography *A Man Called Dash*.) In 1985 my bio/anthology, *The Black Mask Boys* (in which Hammett was prominently featured) was published. Then, in the 1990s, St. Martin's Press published my trilogy of detective thrillers (*The Black Mask Murders, The Marble Orchard*, and *Sharks Never Sleep*) in which Hammett, Chandler, and Erle Stanley Gardner function as amateur sleuths in 1930s Hollywood. (I have Hammett himself narrate the first of these.)

I also wrote extensively about Hammett for *The Armchair Detective*, including three updates to my checklist from *Casebook*.

Which brings us full circle to the critical work of George J. Thompson.

His 1971 dissertation, *The Problem of Moral Vision in Dashiell Hammett's Detective Novels*, written while Thompson was a graduate student at the University of Connecticut, was serialized in seven parts by *The Armchair Detective* from 1973 to 1975. I read it with intense interest as the first extended critical study to deal with Hammett. It struck me as incredibly well done, beautifully researched, and displaying tremendous insight into what made Hammett tick as a writer.

Happily for today's reader, Thompson's work has not dated. Oh, yes, there have been at least seven other full-length critical studies of Hammett published (four of which quote from, and refer to, Thompson's seminal work), but none has surpassed the original. After three decades, Thompson continues to exert a major influence on Hammett criticism, and I recommend his work without reservation. No serious Hammett researcher should miss it.

Even if one might argue with a few of his observations and opinions, Thompson's carefully structured study retains its analytical power and depth. His vision is timeless, and I'm delighted that it is available in hardcover. A worthy effort indeed.

Lastly, what about the subject of this book? What of Dashiell Hammett's influence?

It is pervasive and all-encompassing. The entertainment industry—today's film, television, and ancillary venues— expresses the elements of drama, suspense, and pragmatic reality that Hammett introduced into his fiction. The modern novel carries direct echoes of his realistic approach to scenes, plot, and character. Hammett has emerged as far more than a mystery writer. His work has become an integral part of American culture.

Dashiell Hammett's goal was to win a place in literary history as a major author, beyond the label of "genre writer." Without a doubt, he achieved that goal. (Although, unfortunately, he never realized that he had actually accomplished what he set out to do.)

This fascinating book by George Thompson shows you how Dashiell Hammett did it.

CHAPTER ONE

Hammett's Moral Vision: Three Decades and a Hot Tub Later

THE WRITING OF THIS book came about by what you might consider an incident of good fortune.

As a doctoral student at the University of Connecticut, I had embarked upon a dissertation of the novels by George Meredith. I'd read the entirety of Meredith's novels and letters, and in doing so conceived of a study I sensed would secure me my Ph.D. I began writing and after 100 pages I found myself floundering like a weak swimmer in deep water. I was discovering I didn't much care for Meredith's characters, their plights, or his style of presentation. I felt cloyed, trapped, and disheartened.

Meredith was a bore.

A QUARTERLY JOURNAL DEVOTED TO THE APPRECIATION
OF
MYSTERY, DETECTIVE AND SUSPENSE FICTION
Volume 6   Number 4
August 1973

The second section of Thompson's investigation of
Hammett's novels was serialized in the August 1973 issue
of The Armchair Detective, *volume 6: number 4.*

As an English professor I was then teaching two classes—six hours a week—while seeking to complete the last great hurdle in my five-year Doctoral hunt. I was tired. I'd discovered I'd chosen my subject poorly and I'd had enough of the "graduate experience" to last several dreary lifetimes. One evening, I tossed all I had written into a much-visited downtown garbage can. While walking home I came to believe my doctoral pursuit was over.

Upon reaching home I told my wife what I had done. She was horrified. We had sacrificed much over the past four years, and now had a young infant, little money, and apparently an even lesser future. I bravely told her, "Well, I can always go back to teaching English in high school. . .or I could become an FBI agent."

So much for my verbal judo skills at the time!

Frustrated, and soundly trounced by my less than happy bride, I retreated to a hot tub. I'd snagged a paperback book I rescued the day before while surfing a garage sale. It was Hammett's *Red Harvest*. I read the entire book in one sitting. I became fascinated with the harsh realism of the Op's ventures in Personville/Poisonville. "So much like the revenge tragedies of the Elizabethan and Jacobean eras," I thought out loud. "So unlike the prissy, boring, predictable world of Meredith," I remarked to no one in particular.

[13]

Perhaps, I thought, I might make good use of Hammett to save both my doctorate AND marriage?

The next day, I went to my grim-faced advisor and informed him of my decision to quit Meredith, perhaps, indeed, to settle for the Masters and leave at the end of the semester. I cleverly mentioned toward the end of our meeting that although I knew Dashiell Hammett was not considered part of the typical university canon of approved works, *Red Harvest* had mesmerized me. Perhaps a good study of his novels might prove an atypical scholastic adventure?

I expected to hear a polite guffaw and curt dismissal. Instead, Professor Irving Cummings quietly mused, "You know, I have always thought that. Indeed I have often wished I'd done something on Hammett and the hard-boiled tradition myself."

Hardly believing what I'd just heard, I asked Professor Cummings if he would allow me to read on and develop a workable thesis.

He encouraged me to read all the so-called hardboiled writers. Not only the novels of Hammett, but of Raymond Chandler and Ross Macdonald! Then we could see where we were with a dissertation proposal.

Several weeks later, having read sixteen hours a day, I returned to Professor Cummings' office. I respectfully said, "You know, I could write on all three—Hammett, Chandler, and Macdonald—but I believe there is enough in the Hammett canon for a good dissertation."

He smiled. "I know that, but you had to do your homework on the tradition. Let's do it!"

I owe Dashiell Hammett—and the wise and patient Dr. Cummings—my Ph.D.

Indeed, as you will see, Hammett has shaped my life—as he can yours—in several important ways.

[14]

While teaching at Emporia State University (Kansas), I published my dissertation serially in *The Armchair Detective* journal, commencing in 1973. My academic colleagues were not impressed by my choice, but, like Hammett, I preferred to write for the people who do the work.

I was pleased by the numerous letters of appreciation I received during the 1970s from aficionados of detective literature. Some said I was the first writer to produce an extensive critical analysis of Hammett's fiction and to pay heed to the critical discourse concerning that fiction. I gave presentations on Hammett at several popular culture conventions, but otherwise I was busy teaching and building an academic career during those early years.

Police work, however, interested me. I was still intrigued by the world of the streets I had come to know through the Continental Op and Sam Spade, so I thought, why not see it for myself? In 1975 I became a reserve officer for the Emporia P.D. My academic colleagues again thought I was crazy. Nothing new there!

Another career was born! I loved the streets, the calls for service, and the adrenaline pump that was part of the work I did with the Emporia P.D. I spent more and more of my time riding with officers, finally becoming a Class A Reserve, which meant I could handle my own car and my own beat.

I discovered, much to my amazement, that the officers I worked with—the "old dawgs of the street"—shared a vision very close to that expressed by Hammett in his novels. The JOB and its completion was everything. The thin line between "them" and "us" was just that—thin! The best officers thought like the criminals, but kept their actions ethical. The world we worked in was, as in Hammett's world, unpredictable and unstable. Things never were as they appeared, and no one told you the truth. Deception was a way of life. All you had was yourself, your job knowledge, and your adherence to a larger code of right.

[15]

I found a new "self" emerging from these experiences. I came to understand that randomness is actuality; indeed, uncertainty is the only certainty. Rather than try to control experience—as I had before—I became a participant and an observer of ongoing experience. All you can count on is what you bring to the event.

Police work was, for me, the "beam that fell" and changed my life. The earlier orderly world of academia seemed somehow false. In trying to fit in, I had unwittingly gotten out of step with reality. I very much felt a part of the Sam Spade-Continental Op world depicted in Hammett's novels.

In this new and evolving mode, I discovered something else, too: Effective cops are the best communicators in America! Rhetoric had always been one of my central interests, but no one had ever suggested to me that police officers were consummate rhetoricians. The officers I worked with, some with little or no formal education, were able to talk knives and guns out of people's hands, persuade people to calm down and act rationally, and repeatedly used their words to bring peace out of disorder. I was shocked! The best rhetoricians in the world were street officers! Aristotle would have been proud.

I applied for an extended sabbatical from my university, arguing that "police rhetoric" needed some serious study. Taking another risk, I applied for full-time status with the Emporia P.D. and was accepted. I used my background in classical rhetoric to analyze the skill levels of the officers with whom I worked. I learned "street rhetoric" from them.

In April of 1982, I published an article in the *FBI Bulletin*, "Rhetoric: An Important Tool for Cops," and to my total amazement, over the next six months I received hundreds of letters asking me if I did training in police rhetoric. Taking another risk, I never returned to university teaching. I moved to Albuquerque, New Mexico, shortly thereafter, and founded The Verbal Judo Institute. I developed this new street rhetoric into the full-fledged police-training program now called Verbal Judo.

During the 1980s and 1990s, I spent 300 days a year on the road teaching Verbal Judo or "Tactical Communication" to police departments here in the U.S.A., Canada, and Australia. Verbal Judo is now recognized the as the premiere communication course for people who deal with the public in stressful and unpredictable circumstances, whether they are police officers, federal employees, or business executives.

During these years as I wrote my three books on Verbal Judo I kept in mind Hammett's insistence on being true to reality, the world as it is rather than as I might like it, and tried as best I could to keep my prose taut and muscular—as Hammett might have liked. I had to mirror the realistic edge of the world in which cops work and live. As I look back, my belief in the warrior "code" and my application of it to the modern peace officer comes almost directly from Hammett's works. It is our code that keeps us safe from the folly and greed surrounding us.

To maintain a realistic edge to my presentations, I continued my police work as a reserve with the Sandoval County Sheriff's department near Albuquerque and spent countless hours riding with officers from other departments, from NYPD, LAPD, LA County Sheriffs, Miami Dade P.D., and Chicago P.D., to Federal agencies such as the National Service, Forest Service, and DEA. Again, people thought I was crazy to spend time in such dangerous environments, but to me, it was the only way I could come to understand the "truth" of police work. I had to be competent in the job to preach to other officers how best to do it.

I now see, after all these years, that I followed, in my own way, the philosophy of the Continental Op and Sam Spade as I had defined it in my dissertation: Know the real world, deal with the enemy dispassionately, and above all, win with integrity to your own code. Hammett's detectives were warriors in a corrupt world. The Op and Spade were manhunters. They had their own code that kept them from falling to the greed and folly of those around them.

Just as Sam Spade had to be different from his world to bring the corrupt to justice, so, too, do today's police have to be unlike the people they serve if they are to complete the job tasks assigned. As the "Thin Blue Line" between order and disorder, peace and violence, officers must essentially be better

[17]

and "unlike" those with whom they interact. To be effective, they may appear to be "like" those with whom they deal, but that is an illusion.

The code of the Peace Warrior, as we preach it in Verbal Judo, is bifurcated: Talk the talk of peace, but be prepared to respond to violence should force be necessary. Use words to redirect and calm, wherever and whenever possible. Model peace by your own behavior. But, should violence be unavoidable, be ready to employ physical skills with devastating, yet restrained, precision. Officers have always had formal training in the physical arts, but never, before Verbal Judo, in the verbal arts. In today's world, realism dictates that a formal, tactical approach to communication is necessary. I have tried to fill that void.

I now see, thirty years later, that my immersion in Dashiell Hammett's world created a state of mind I have carried with me ever since. As Joe Gores, on page 127 of his paper "Dashiell Hammett" in *AZ Murder Goes Classic: Papers of the Conference* (Scottsdale: Poisoned Pen Press, 1997), suggests of Hammett:

> He was not a writer learning about private detection in order to create a detective hero; he was a detective learning about writing in order to make a living. This meant that as he wrote, he retained the detective's subconscious attitudes toward life.

My police experience, both as an actor and as an observer, has validated my thinking about Hammett's fictional detectives. The world of the streets is indeed "mean," unpredictable, and threatening to any good man who might try to make a difference. My professorial view, in 1972, of Hammett's Personville in *Red Harvest* was that its landscape was extreme. With my police experience, I no longer believe this to be so. Today's world is so corrupt—from drive-by shootings and mass murders to corporate lies and the "forked-tongues" of our elected representatives—Person-Poisonville seems an all too familiar landscape. The greed and folly of the characters in *The Maltese Falcon* now seem ubiquitous and commonplace, and even Nick's hedonistic stance in *The Thin Man* is understandable, if not entirely likeable.

The Peace Warrior we try to train in Verbal Judo must, I now see, have the very qualities of a Continental Op or a Sam Spade. Our model policeman must, above all, be professional. He is not hired to express his or her personal feelings; instead, he or she is expected to be a walking enactment of the law. A "hard-boiled" exterior is indeed necessary to help officers handle the harshness of the outside world and the psychological pressure the various calls for duty exert on them as they work the streets. But it is also necessary to protect the inner self, the self of integrity and ethical conduct. In *The Thin Man*, Hammett's darkening authorial vision ends with Nick Charles, whose "hard-boiled" stance is only that—a stance, devoid of meaningful connection with his internal self. In Nick, *doing* and *being* are forever disjoined, forever separated from dynamic and meaningful connection, and Hammett's vision closes on that note.

[19]

In our Verbal Judo training, however, we try to show officers they can conduct themselves authentically, and not drift into the cynicism and lack of commitment of a Nick Charles. We offer a series of strategies and tactics that enable officers to stay calm under pressure, focus on the goal of the discourse, and succeed in redirecting hostility into more peaceable channels. We teach officers to think that their quintessential job is to "think for people as they might think for themselves 48 to 72 hours later," without the present influences of liquor, drugs, or rage. Good officers "protect" people from themselves and others, and they "serve" by thinking for others as those others might think under better conditions. The officers are taught that the "Peace Warrior" is essentially *a protector,* a protector of the weak, the innocent, and yes, even the guilty—those who must nevertheless be brought to justice. I believe this is a vision that can keep officers motivated and free from the pitfalls of cynicism and pervasive ennui that entrapped Nick Charles and perhaps Hammett himself.

Had Vince Emery not contacted me about publishing my manuscript on Hammett, I do not know if I would have realized Hammett's influence on my present work with Verbal Judo. I now see the mindset I developed while immersed in Hammett became part and parcel of the mindset I used on the street as a police officer, and with slight changes, became the mindset I teach young officers in Verbal Judo.

As I reread my own work, now thirty years later, I am more convinced then ever that the world we live in needs hard-boiled operatives to right the wrongs and act when others will not, or cannot. That gray area, which is "the thin blue line" between the forces of good and the forces of evil, that area where the moral and ethical well-intentioned operative must work his magic, is today even more problematic than in Hammett's era. The good officer must know what laws can be bent, and how far, without breaking, and the good undercover officer must appear more corrupt than he is to be effective with those with whom he deals.

Knowing the risks of policing in today's society led me to make the mascot of Verbal Judo training the chameleon, that wonderful subtle little beast that can change its coloring to blend with its environment to survive and win the game of life. No doubt my immersion in Hammett's fiction, with its portrayal of Spade's and the Op's antics and gamesmanship, led me in this direction. Like the chameleon, street officers have to be flexible and capable of changing as the situations change. They have to wear a variety of faces to meet the faces they meet. They must look pleasant on one call when they may not feel at all pleasant, or intimidating when fearful at the next call. Ultimately, the must always have the skill of becoming who they have to be to handle the situation in front of them. Anything less is disaster. Role-playing and emotional distance is the secret of winning. Like Sam Spade, who tells Brigid, "I do hate being hit without hitting back...but it's a cheap enough price to pay for winning," officers must keep distance and maintain a professional perspective if they are to win.

During my hundreds of hours working with successful officers in the big cities, I came to admire their work as I admired Sam Spade in *The Maltese Falcon*. Many of the officers, torn between the corruption of the streets and the uncertain backing and support from their own highly politicized departments, discovered that adherence to the job was their only salvation. These officers, dedicated as they were to doing the right thing, used their own integrity as a basis of action, as did Sam Spade. Like Spade, they focused on the job. Each job provided a beginning, middle, and end and thus became a way for them to hold onto reality. Ironically, to be successful in their jobs, these officers had to, like Spade, become "unlike" all others in their world, from the criminals they pursue to the departments they represent.

I argue in my chapter on *The Maltese Falcon*, that Hammett's rendering of Sam Spade shows that a moral man can act in a corrupt world without himself becoming corrupted or infected, but admittedly, the price is high. The hero is left with skepticism and alienation from those he serves. So, too, with all too many of today's better officers. They will tell you they feel alienated from their departments, and skeptical about the efficacy of the law and the court system. Only the pursuit of the individual job(s) and the tight fellowship they feel with their

[21]

team members keeps them uplifted and motivated. The enjoy-ment lies in the "game" itself. The trick, as it was for Spade, is to keep integrity and focus as the game is played out.

Hammett's stress that police work and detection is at best a serious game, played according to the rules the world depicted will allow, helped me keep perspective during my own street work. I recall often thinking of Hammett's stress on knowing the world, as it is, not falling to romantic visions that might make us feel better. I clearly remember one officer complaining to me after a particularly difficult court case that our prosecu-tor was having a beer the next night with the defense counsel! "How can they be friends?" he wanted to know. Had this officer read his Hammett he would have known it's all a game; the roles in court are just that, roles. Not long after that that the officer quit, later explaining that the system wasn't aboveboard and fair. Hammett would have had a laugh at that, as did I.

Certainly one of the things that make Hammett's fiction "real" is its pragmatic thrust—get the job done and win.

Again and again, the Op and Sam Spade do things to the bad guys we wish we could do. Our "willing suspension of disbelief" allows us to marvel at the stratagems employed by the Op and Spade, and it provides us with a wonderful cathar-sis of poetic justice. The crooks always get what's coming to them and, more often than not, they entrap or kill themselves through their greed, vanity, and foolishness. We as readers love it! Hammett's opting to use detectives rather than police to operate in the dark world of crime and corruption makes won-derful sense because the detective has much greater latitude in deciding what rules to bend, even break, to accomplish the task of cleansing the infected landscapes and bringing to justice those who so righteously deserve it.

In all, as I reread my work on Hammett's novels, I stand by what I have written. My police work and my police training have deepened my appreciation of Hammett's fictional detectives in their struggle to right the wrongs so prevalent in their world. Hammett meant us, I believe, to take his Op and Sam Spade as realistic figures trying to do a job, not just as allegorical representations.

Seen this way, Hammett does, as I argue in this book, present us with a progressive analysis of a developing and evolving moral vision. As readers, we share in the increasing difficulties faced by an ethical and moral operative trying to do a job in a corrupt and morally bankrupt world. His novels make for great reading and, as I have found by my own experiences, the good operative does not have to end in rejection of his world or in cynical withdrawal.

I've often thought that the modern Peace Warrior we teach and define would have appealed to Dashiell Hammett's realistic sense of what it might actually take to work ethically in a corrupt world. At least, I like to think so.

The original versions of George J. Thompson's chapters about
The Dain Curse, The Maltese Falcon, The Glass Key, *and*
The Thin Man *appeared in these four issues of* The Armchair
Detective *from November 1973 to November 1974.*

CHAPTER TWO

Moral Vision:
What and Why

T<small>HE SIX NOVELS</small> <small>BY</small> Dashiell Hammett—*Blood Money* (1927, published 1942), *Red Harvest* (1929), *The Dain Curse* (1929), *The Maltese Falcon* (1930), *The Glass Key* (1931), and *The Thin Man* (1934)—have all at one time or another received critical attention and varying degrees of acclaim. What is lacking, however, is an in-depth study of any one of the novels and a coherent analysis of the novels as a whole.

The result so far, therefore, is that we have only a partial knowledge of Dashiell Hammett's literary expression in any one novel, and an equally incomplete view of him as an artist. Does he mature as a novelist from *Red Harvest* through *The Thin Man* or not? Is there a point in his career where we can say that he is at his best? Do his interests and themes remain constant, or does he vary his focus as he moves from novel to novel? Has he wedded his social and moral vision to his form successfully? Such questions have either not been asked or satisfactorily answered, and it is the purpose of this study to develop a coherent view of the meaning and significance of Dashiell Hammett's novels.

I will focus in detail on five novels (excluding *Blood Money*) and show that if we focus on Hammett's rendering of his protagonists, we find a clear and definitive progression of man's potential to deal morally and ethically with decadent worlds.

I chose moral vision as my unifying conception because it demands at least a three-part approach to the novels. To determine what, if any, the moral vision is in a Hammett novel, it is necessary to analyze the way in which he portrays the quality of his hero, the kind of world he shows the hero acting in, and the various kinds of resolutions that are possible in such a world. The moral quality of a protagonist can be defined accurately only if we measure his behavior in terms of the kinds of choices he makes and look to the motives of those choices. His moral rectitude may be determined, as well, by comparing his actions and motives for acting with the other characters in the work and by clearly determining the nature of the world in which such action takes place. If, for example, the hero's world offers a limited number of viable possibilities, then this fact must be taken into consideration in any evaluation of his moral worth.

Such an approach forces us to go beyond the easy generalizations critics find so applicable to Hammett's work and to examine in depth their validity. We may discover that the generalizations hold, in which case we can be more properly certain about them; but it may be that the generalizations are only partial, that there is a complexity in Hammett's novels that is too often obscured by such abstractions, in which case, a specific and detailed examination can only help to present a more balanced and informed view.

It is virtually commonplace to assume that the Hammett world is a demonic world of violence, almost grimly Jacobean in atmosphere. Hammett places his heroes in the thick of squalor and violence and, with the exception of Ned Beaumont in *The Glass Key*, his hero is a professional detective assigned (directly or indirectly) the task of searching out the truth and cleaning up what he can of the stew of corruption.

A critic such as George Grella, for instance, describes the Hammett world as an allegorical representation of America the moral wasteland, a place in which the detective concerned with right and wrong can only turn inward, alienated from all he sees around him.[1] Elsewhere, Grella says that the tough guy hero is in open rebellion against society, holding on only to "solipsistic faith in his own competency."[2] A similar perception probably led Robert Edenbaum to this remark about the Hammett hero:

> Instead of the potential despair of Hemingway, Hammett gives you the unimpaired control and machine-like efficiency: the tough guy refuses "to place himself in a position to lose." For all (or most) intents and purposes the inner world does not exist: the mask is the self. It is that "voluntary mutilation" of life that is the subject of these novels as much as Hemingway's stoical mask is his.[3]

Another critic calls Hammett's *Red Harvest* a "synecdoche for a ruined America."[4] Again and again what critics see in Hammett's fictional world is moral breakdown, fragmentation, and dissolution of any and all external values. What is left, they argue, is the tough guy *Weltanschauung*. Leslie Fiedler describes the Hammett detective as

> the cowboy adapted to life on the city streets, the embodiment of innocence moving untouched through universal guilt. As created by Dashiell, Hammett, the blameless shamus is also the honest proletarian, illuminating decadent society of the rich.[5]

The problem with such descriptions, however, is their over-simplification. It is highly questionable, for example, if Fiedler can rightly assume the innocence of Hammett's private eyes when they themselves are unable to take such an agreeable view. Moreover, as I will show, there is good reason to believe that Hammett himself did not take such a sanguine view of his creations. Edenbaum is certainly closer to the truth when he speaks of voluntary mutilation as being the subject for Hammett's works, but unfortunately he leaves it at that and does not examine the full significance of his insight.

As early as 1944, André Gide put his finger on one of the most singularly striking elements of Hammett's representation of society: the depiction of deception as a way of life. Referring to *Red Harvest* in particular, Gide speaks of "dialogues, in which every character is trying to deceive all the others and in which the truth slowly becomes visible through a fog of deception."[6] Such description fits all of Hammett's novels from *Red Harvest* to *The Thin Man*. Of course, a world permeated by deception is an ambiguous world. Given the world, the hero's portrayal will necessarily be ambiguous also. Henry Parkes suggests one such ambiguity when he says

> the private eye avenges crime but is invariably regarded as a suspicious character by the district attorney and the

officers of the homicide bureau. Objectively, the hero is defending civilization, yet at the same time civilization is repressive and corrupting.[7]

The notion that society is itself corrupting is found everywhere in Hammett's work, but a larger and more informing ambiguity is the entire problem of an honest man acting at all in such a deceptive world. Like Hamlet, to be at all effective, the private eye must be a pragmatist. He must be able to adopt masks and pretend to be other than he is. He must walk down mean streets, meeting meanness at every corner. How to keep from being tarnished? This is the interesting moral question, and a troublesome one with respect to Hammett's heroes. The Hammett hero gets the assigned task done, but at considerable cost to himself. Unlike the traditional detective story in which crime is portrayed as a temporary aberration in an otherwise orderly universe and in which the detective's actions are shown to restore his society to health, the Hammett novels render an extremely ambiguous moral vision. Endings occur, but leave questions lingering in the mind of the reader concerning the nature and role of the private eye. With perhaps one exception, none of the novels leaves one with the sense that the heroic task has been heroically completed (a theme so familiar in the traditional genre) or that the world is appreciably better off for the actions of the protagonist.

[29]

Yet it would be a mistake to try to divorce Hammett's work from the genre of crime fiction and the detective story. I conceive of Hammett's work as being more about a detective and his world than a detective story, but all five major novels are unmistakably related to the detective form. In each there is something to be discovered. In *Red Harvest* the discovery question moves from the problems of who killed Donald Willsson and Dinah Brand to the larger question: how can the centers of power be destroyed?

In *The Dain Curse* the discovery issues are again multiple and progressive: Who stole Edgar Leggett's diamonds? Who is trying to harm Gabrielle Leggett? Who killed Eric Collinson? In *The Maltese Falcon* the initial question is who killed Sam Spade's partner, Miles Archer , and this is enlarged to include two other related questions: the extent of Brigid O'Shaughnessy's complicity and the whereabouts and value of the Maltese Falcon. *The Glass Key* concentrates on the question of Paul Madvig's guilt or innocence in the murder of Taylor Henry. *The Thin Man* involves Nick Charles in the problem of who killed Julia Wolf and later, who killed Clyde Wynant.

Yet as every reader of Hammett realizes, such summary statements are hardly sufficient to explain the genuine power and authenticity of vision in these novels. The puzzle of detection is central to all five, but in each we feel that the process of discovery leads to more than an answer to a riddle. As I intend to show, Hammett's repeated use of multiple cases that proliferate into and connect each other and his stress on the increasing complexity and proliferation of criminal culpability suggests his interest in writing serious detective novels, novels that hold the reader's attention not only because they spin ingenious and mystifying plots, but because they also probe such questions as the nature of modern society, the moral and ethical man's viability in such a society, and the larger, more informing question of what it means to be an authentic self in twentieth-century America.

Admittedly, such issues are rarely thought central to the detective genre and some argue that such questions are impossible to explore in any depth whatsoever in such a genre. This study does, in part, examine the validity of such assertions. One of the premises of my approach is that Hammett was an artist, concerned with questions of art and artistry, and one who consistently experimented with form and content in an attempt to transcend the traditional parameters of the form by extending the range, the scope, and the meaning of detection.

Hammett, himself, more than once expressed a seriousness about his writing rarely heard, at least until then, from writers of detective fiction. In a letter in 1928, he writes:

> I am one of the few... people moderately literate who take the detective story seriously... Some day some-body's going to make "literature" of it.[8]

At this time, Hammett had not had a novel published; a year later, however, he produced two, *Red Harvest* and *The Dain Curse*, and in the next four years came his major achievements, *The Maltese Falcon*, *The Glass Key*, and *The Thin Man*. To one degree or another, each novel reflects his attempts to discover ways to harmonize his vision and his form, ways to add depth of meaning and resonance to his detective plots, and ways to express his own very personal vision of many and his world.

Hammett himself said:

> The contemporary novelist's job is to take pieces of life and arrange them on paper, and the more direct their passage from street to paper the more lifelike they should turn out.
>
> The contemporary novel, it seems to me, needs tempo—not to cram into each page as many things as possible—but to make what is set down seem *truly contemporary*, to give the impression of things happening *here and now*, to force upon the reader a feeling of *immediacy*.... [The writer] must know how things happen—not how they are remembered in later years—and he must write them down that way.[9]

[31]

In these lines Hammett makes it clear that writing is a serious endeavor. To him it is a matter of accurate selection and careful arrangement, with the controlling purpose being to create an illusion of immediacy. He implies that an artist must know his world experientially if he is to describe it realistically. With such a philosophy it is hardly surprising that he would choose the detective genre as his artistic medium. Over a seven-year period interrupted by military service and hospitalization, his four or five years as a Pinkerton's detective gave him his material, but finding the right way to use this experience was his ongoing concern.

Early evaluations by Anthony Boucher and Raymond Chandler demonstrate that Hammett had moved beyond the run-of-the-mill detective formulas so prevalent in his day. Boucher argued that

> In only a decade of creativity Hammett exerted an influence on the American detective story greater than that of any author since Poe.[10]

and Chandler pointed out, perhaps more tendentiously, that

> Hammett gave murder back to the kind of people that commit it for reasons, not just to provide a corpse.... He was spare, frugal, hardboiled, but he did over and over again what only the best writers can ever do at all. He wrote scenes that seemed never to have been written before.[11]

The majority of critics express similar sentiments, but though such praise may be well placed, it does not substantially increase our knowledge of Hammett as an artist. We know that Hammett's style and form has been imitated and expanded, especially by Raymond Chandler and Ross Macdonald, and it is very clear that he has achieved a reputation as an innovator and discoverer of a new form.

Yet even Raymond Chandler, who was one of Hammett's most ardent admirers, failed to perceive the full complexity and artistry in his work. Too often what ones comes away with after reading the critical material on Hammett—reviews, critiques, and analyses—are the stereotypical notions that he was the founder of the so-called hardboiled detective story, that his style is sparse, hard, muscular, realistic prose, and that his heroes are coldly methodical, machine-like creations.

One does not need to deny such generalizations to say that they may be unfair or misleading. A very real problem with such summations of Hammett's skill is that they encourage us to see him as a static writer, repeatedly employing the same formulas in only slightly varying patterns.

Surprisingly, within these generally accepted notions there is a great deal of disagreement over the worth of any one of his novels. The greatest unanimity in evaluation is on *The Maltese Falcon*—most consider it his best—but this is not universally granted. As for the others, there is very little critical harmony.

A central purpose of this study is to offer a reading of the five novels that will clarify Hammett's particular aims and intentions in each, and at the same time establish the validity of the assertion that one can see a developing artistic pattern of moral and social vision as one moves from *Red Harvest* through *The Thin Man*, a pattern that suggests not only Hammett's growth as an artist and his expansiveness of vision, but that may enable us to explain why, following *The Thin Man*, he ceased writing serious fiction.

Red Harvest *was published February 1, 1929. According to rare bookseller and Hammett bibliographer Mark Sutcliffe, a copy of an unsigned first edition, first printing in very good plus to near fine condition in a similar condition dust jacket would be worth $40,000 to $60,000 today. A copy in truly fine condition would be worth more.*

CHAPTER THREE

Red Harvest:
The Pragmatic and
Moral Dilemma

R ED *HARVEST* (1929) ORIGINALLY appeared in *Black Mask*,
November 1927-February 1928, as a series of four complete adventures. The editor of *Black Mask*, Joseph T. Shaw,
described the series as "dealing with a city whose administra-
tors have gone mad with power and lust of wealth. It is, to our
minds, the ideal detective story—the new type of fiction which
Black Mask is seeking to develop."[1]

William Nolan describes Hammett's reworking of the four
sections into the novel *Red Harvest* and argues that at least
on the technical level, the novel "reflects Hammett's careful
approach to the novel form, his attention to the smallest detail

[35]

in dialogue and description."[2] I would go even farther by suggesting that despite the novel's episodic nature, Hammett has skillfully created a unified effect of moral vision by placing his protagonist squarely in the middle of the action and by having the action reflect not only upon the moral worth of the denizens of Personville but also upon the Continental Op as well.

As Dashiell Hammett's first unified novel,[3] *Red Harvest* provides an interesting test case for a theory about the ambiguity of moral vision because it seems the simplest and most straightforward in character and action. George Grella calls the protagonist the "simple Op,"[4] and Robert Edenbaum says "The moral opposites are clear-cut," and that the Op's "immunity from corruption and temptation" indicates something about the allegorical nature of" the novel.[5] A rather different view is offered by William Kenney, who argues that the Continental Op is "morally ineffectual and morally ambiguous," and that he is himself "involved in the corruption that pervades his world."[6] A few lines later, however, Kenney remarks that "professionalism becomes a substitute for morality" to the Op, thereby suggesting that a code (non-moral) is being followed and adhered to with some loyalty.[7] There is, then, some disagreement, and a close analysis of the action may help to clarify the matter.

[36]

Hammett indicates the nature of Personville very early in the novel. More appropriately called Poisonville, it

> . . . wasn't pretty. Most of the builders had gone in for gaudiness. Maybe they had been successful at first. Since then the smelters whose brick stacks stuck up tall against a gloomy mountain to the south had yellow-smoked everything into uniform dinginess. The result was an ugly city of forty thousand people, set in an ugly notch between two ugly mountains that

had been all dirtied up by mining. Spread over this was a grimy sky that looked as if it had come out of the smelters' stacks.[8]

The industrial nature of the town has blighted surrounding nature. Like the town, the people are shabby and rumpled in appearance, and dull and grey of eye. Into this dying landscape comes the Op, employed by Donald Willsson for a job which is not made immediately clear because Donald is killed before the Op can talk with him.

That violence is a part of the Personville world even before the Op arrives is an important fact to consider as we attempt to arrive at some kind of evaluation of him. Hammett lets the action speak for itself; we are introduced to the shabby and ugly world of Personville in the first few paragraphs of the novel, and the first action we hear about is the murder of Donald Willsson. The town's history is sketched for us by labor union organizer Bill Quint, whose narrative makes it clear that its shabbiness is not merely external; the city is sick from the disease of violence, greed, and capitalistic extortion. For forty years, we are told, Elihu Willsson "has owned Personville, heart, soul, skin and guts."[9] His corrupt, tyrannical leadership precipitated a miner's strike which lasted eight months:

> Both sides bled plenty. The wobblies had to do their own bleeding. Old Elihu hired gunmen, strike-break-ers, national guardsmen and even parts of the regular army, to do his. When the last skull had been cracked, the last rib kicked in, organized labor in Personville was a used firecracker.[10]

Elihu Willsson's greed is coupled with absolute power, and the little man bleeds. But Elihu's violence breeds more violence:

> To beat the miners he had to let his hired thugs run wild. When the fight was over he couldn't get rid of them. He had given his city to them, and he wasn't strong enough to take it away from them. Personville looked good to them and they took it over. They had won his strike for him and they took the city for their spoils. He couldn't openly break with them. They had too much on him. He was responsible for all they had done during the strike.[11]

Elihu's operation backfires—his thugs now rule—and he thinks he has but one last hope: his son. He brings Donald back to Personville and gives him full charge of the city's newspapers, the *Morning Herald* and the *Evening Herald*. He uses his son to get back at the gangsters, and his son is killed.

Such is the situation when the Op enters Personville, and this background is essential in understanding both the nature of the town and the Op's actions from this point. In a single chapter Hammett has indicated that Personville is a poisonous world, and world run by heartless machiavels like old Elihu who thinks nothing of using thugs to butcher miners and his son to rid himself of the thugs. Violence and power seem to be the only visible forces in a world controlled by an unholy trinity of gangsters, corrupt politicians, and a corrupt chief of police. Like Robert Edenbaum, William Nolan stresses the allegorical nature of *Red Harvest*.

[38]

> As Dante used his native Florence as a model for hell, as Dickens depicted the horrors of London with its lust, poverty and crime, as Melville projected his gothic-vision of New York as "an inferno into which the hero falls"—so Hammett utilized Poisonville.[12]

Any judgment of the Continental Op must take into consideration this allegorical typography. Hammett stresses the Personville-Poisonville connection throughout the novel, and he means for us to evaluate his hero's actions with this landscape in mind. As we will see, one of the central tensions in this novel is between this allegorical landscape and the Op's actions within it, the situation as it is and the situation that the Op creates.

The specific reason Donald Willsson has sent for the Op is left purposefully vague by Hammett. We are only told that he had "some work" for him, and the Op decides the least he can do is to find out who killed his client. But Elihu intrudes, ostensibly to hire him for a clear-cut job: "to clear this pig-sty of Poisonville for me, to smoke out the rats, little and big."[13] The Op's code of ethics is nowhere made clearer than the terms he sets for agreeing to the proposal:

> "I'd have to have a free hand—no favors to anybody—run the job as I pleased. . . . But I'm not playing politics for you. I'm not hiring out to help you kick them back in line—with the job being called off then. If you want the job done you'll plank down enough money to pay for a complete job. Any that's left over will be returned to you. But you're going to get a complete job or nothing. That's the way it'll have to be. Take it or leave it."[14]

[39]

This is the Op's declaration of professionalism of which Kenney speaks. He's a pro; it's all or nothing, and it will be a complete job, run as he sees fit. He makes it clear he will not be Elihu's puppet; he will be his own man. Ironically, Elihu gives the Op exactly the kind of power and freedom Donald would have probably tried to give the Op had the lived, and Elihu also unwittingly sets the Op on the mission that will eventually bring him down as king of Personville.

By chapter seven the Op has discovered the killer of Donald Willsson. The Op's method of breaking Robert Albury down and leading him to confess he is the murderer is typical of his method throughout the novel; and Albury's motivation for his crime is likewise typical of the other motives for action we see throughout the novel. The Albury episode serves as a prototype incident for the main plot, and thus functions as a representational technique. Charles McLaughlin has pointed out that the

> plot of mimetic work is not a sequence of *any* probable incidents, but rather a sequence of incidents which effect some important change in the protagonist (Fortune, Character, Thought) and which, as a consequence, have the power to move out emotions in a certain way.[15]

If we accept this view of plot, we can more readily see how the Albury episode is purely representational: it does not effect any change in the Op's behavior. It does, however, serve to illustrate how pervasive greed and corruption are in Personville. Albury kills Donald because, as he says,

> "All I could think about was that I had lost her because I had no more money, and he was taking five thousand dollars to her. It was the check. Can you understand that? . . . It was seeing the check—and knowing that I'd lost her because my money was gone."[16]

Albury mistakenly assumes Donald had taken Dinah Brand away from him because he took a large check to her. Value is measured solely in dollars in Personville, and if you don't have it, you react violently. Both Albury's failure to interpret correctly what he sees and his motive for murder are consistent with the conditions of Personville. Deception, violence, and money are the staples of Poisonville.

The Albury episode serves yet another function: it characterizes the Op and his methods. His psychological insight is made very clear in his confrontation with Albury. He was too calm, so "I had to be nasty," says the Op. "I made myself sneer at him. . . I let him have the other barrel."[17] The Op plays the nasty role in order to get under Albury's skin:

> I had to get under your skin, and that was the best way
> I knew. The way you'd talked about the girl showed
> me you were too good an actor to be broken down by
> straight hammering.[18]

He reads people well and is flexible in his approach. He is capable of adopting a role, a mask, in order to probe a man's weakness, and this proves to be his method throughout the main action.

Through the first seven chapters, then, Hammett has drawn a unified picture of a diseased world. Unity of tone is achieved by the suggestion that all the characters in Personville—with the exception of the Op—proceed from one set of values: greed and what we might call Machiavellian policy. Greed is central, the dominant passion, and Machiavellian policy is the generally accepted means. Whether it is Elihu's greed for power and total control, or police chief John Noonan's desire for additional power, or the gangsters' desire for control of the city, or Albury's desire to possess Dinah, or even Dinah's own lust for dollars for power—whatever the particular manifestation, the basic motivation is greed, and the game everybody plays is power politics. Hammett's use of perspective to create unity of

[41]

tone suggests nothing quite so much as certain Jacobean tragedies. Consider, for example, Robert Ornstein's description of
Cyril Tourneur's technique for rendering a dramatic universe
in *The Revenger's Tragedy*:

> Tourneur cannot convince us that his tragic universe
> holds a mirror up to nature, but he skillfully creates
> an illusion of depth in his two-dimensional scene by
> suggesting that the Duke's court extends and merges
> imperceptibly with a larger world which, if brought into
> the foreground, would be no different from the group
> of sensualists which Tourneur examines in detail.[19]

Throughout *Red Harvest* Hammett suggests precisely this kind
of pervasive moral decadence by incorporating into the main
action shadowy, peripheral characters who, though they may
appear only once or twice, are nevertheless useful in intimating
the general atmosphere of corruption surrounding the action.

Robert Albury, a nondescript bank teller who just happens to be one of the many men caught in Dinah's scheme for
money, is one such example. Bill Quint, who we learn has also
been pulled in by Dinah's lures, is another. The list of men she
has had at one time or another entrapped stretches from Elihu
himself to the little people, the Quints and Alburys.

Perhaps more impressive, however, is the use Hammett
makes of such unmemorable figures as Shepp and Vanaman,
Ike Bush, Myrtle Jennison, Bob MacSwain, and Charles Proctor Dawn. Though we are shown that Chief Noonan in no
better than a gangster, Hammett uses the two cops, Shepp and
Vanaman, to suggest that all policeman, from the biggest to
the smallest, are out for personal gain. They arrive at Dinah
Brand's apartment after her murder and abscond with her
jewelry and her "hot" letters implicating Elihu in a sordid love

affair. Charles Proctor Dawn, the corrupt lawyer who tries to blackmail the Op, is the one to whom Shepp and Vanaman give the letters in the hope that a profit can be made by blackmailing Elihu. When Dawn is killed, Shepp and Vanaman flee, never to be heard of again. Even sports in Personville are rigged by gamblers and the only participants are bums—like Kid Cooper—and fugitives from the law, like Ike Bush, who is just another example of someone living a life of deception and crime. People like the ex-cop Bob MacSwain, the jealous killer of Tim Noonan, live in fear of Chief Noonan, and to save his own neck MacSwain constructs a web of lies implicating Max Thaler as the murderer of Tim. Lastly, Myrtle Jennison, friend of the gambler Thaler, thinking he killed Tim, propositions MacSwain with money to cover up the killing by making it appear suicide.

Each of these cases illustrates some mole of infection: families disintegrate, like Noonan's, as his wife goes off to play around with his brother Tim; police ranks are filled by self-seekers; fugitives from justice are social attractions; crimes are made to look like accidents; and legal expertise becomes leverage for blackmail and extortion. The main characters are equally corrupt. The plot pits the Continental Op against the gambler Max Thaler, the corrupt police Chief Noonan and his cohorts, and the other gang leaders, Pete the Finn, Reno Starkey, and Lew Yard. Ironically, near the end, even the Op's employer, Elihu, becomes an antagonist. It is Hammett's use, however, of the peripheral characters which creates the illusion of depth in his two-dimensional scene. With the possible exception of the Op, alternatives to corrupt behavior are nowhere to be seen, as they are, for example, in a Jacobean play with a similar theme: *Sejanus: His Fall*. In this play, Ben Jonson uses his minor figures to voice the old values, the moral values, but they provide little relief because Jonson's emphasis is on their total impotence.

[43]

People in *Red Harvest* seem unaware of other possible modes of behavior. They have all been poisoned, morally.

The Continental Op makes no grand moral speeches, but he does appear to be a man of his word, one committed to a personal code of ethics. He seems an anomaly in the Poisonville world because, as well as having a code, he possesses a conscience: "On the way down to the City Hall with the boy and the gun I apologized for the village cut-up stuff I had put in the early part of the shake-down. . . ."[20] At the same time, as we saw in his shrewd psychological attack on Albury, he is well equipped to deal with the deceptive world of Personville. It is easy to agree with Robert Edenbaum at this point that the "moral oppositions are clear-cut." They seem to be. The Op stands on something solid—his professionalism—and though it is more amoral than moral, it is at least something to look to in a world that is otherwise dark and deceptive.

But I do not think it remains this simple. Kenney's statement that the Continental Op is "himself involved in the corruption that pervades his world" deserves a detailed examination. If we are to arrive, in fact, at a definition of Hammett's moral vision, we must determine whether his protagonist remains constant, or changes, and if the latter, define precisely what the nature of that change is and be able to formulate criteria by which to evaluate it.

When the Op discovers that Albury killed Elihu Willsson's son, Donald, Elihu asks him to call his job finished: "The check I gave you last night. . . is only fair pay for the work you have done."[21] But the Op adheres to his earlier definition of what the job was to be:

> "I'll give you nothing except a good job of city-cleaning. That's what you bargained for, and that's what you're going to get. You know now that your son was killed by

young Albury, and not by your playmates. They know now that Thaler wasn't helping you double-cross them. With your son dead, you've been able to promise them that the newspapers won't dig up any more dirt. All's lovely and peaceful again."[22]

The Op won't allow any shuffling of purpose; he sees clearly that old Elihu hopes to go on as if nothing had happened. But the job-ethic is not the only force that influences the Op's decision to go on with the job:

> "Your fat chief of police tried to assassinate me last night. I don't like that. I'm just mean enough to want to ruin him for it. Now I'm going to have my fun. I've got ten thousand dollars of your money to play with. I'm going to use it opening Poisonville up from Adam's apple to ankles."[23]

He is determined not only because he gave his word that he would do a particular job; the earlier attempt by Chief Noonan to catch him in crossfire between police and gangsters has gotten his blood up. Through the first seven chapters, the action he participates in exerts an influence over him; he now wants to strike back. Hammett's diction suggests that the Op's motive for staying in Personville is not merely a matter of professional ethics. The Op talks about his "fun" and using Elihu's money "to play with," word that imply a personal glee in taking revenge.

The importance of noticing the slight alteration in the Op's motive for acting is not that we are given ground to condemn him. Far from it. Our response to the decision to go on with the job can only be approval. Hammett has so shaped events in the first seven chapters that almost any motive for cleaning up the sty of Personville would seem appropriate, but at the same time he has suggested an ambiguity of motives and tendencies within his protagonist. The Op is a man who has a code, but he is also one who has exhibited a propensity to become caught up in the action, to become personally involved in feelings that have little to do with professional codes of ethics. In so doing, Hammett has made his hero more human, and more vulnerable.

Hammett emphasizes the Op's commitment to the more personal motive in the very next chapter:

> "I don't like the way Poisonville has treated me. I've got my chance now, and I'm going to even up...There was a time when I wanted to be let alone. If I had been, maybe now I'd be riding back to San Francisco. But I wasn't. Especially I wasn't let alone by that fat Noonan. He's had two tries at my scalp in two days. That's plenty. Now it's my turn to run him ragged, and that's exactly what I'm going to do. Poisonville is ripe for the harvest. It's a job I like, and I'm going to it."[24]

Hammett portrays his protagonist as a man caught between two extremes: the legal and the personal. The above lines on the one hand, are reminiscent of the *lex talionis*[25] code: even up, blood for blood. The *Harvest* of revenge promises to be *Red*. Nowhere does the Op talk about law or justice in this vow; the matter is partly a personal one. The detective now seems to represent himself more than his client, and yet his personal stand implies a social, even moral, perspective as well. The Op's emphasis is on a cleaning up, a harvesting of rottenness and corruption. The harvest image suggests a natural, if not a moral, necessity for action. From his point of view, Noonan has begun the dirty play, and deserves retribution. Noonan is the first necessary step to the larger goal of destroying the whole corrupt power structure of the town.

Again, the argument is not that the Op is a negative figure, only a vulnerable one. Open to falling morally and ethically in our eyes, the Op becomes an interesting character in his own right. Critics have generally ignored this aspect of his character. A critical argument against seeing the Op as I do might advance the assertion that a reader can only import his own values into the novel because morality and ethics are not stressed by Hammett. Further, the argument might go, the Op himself has never talked in moral terms, so why should anyone presume morality has any place in his character? I am willing to grant immediately that the Op's code seems amoral; it seems purely a matter of doing a job, and therefore we must partially judge him on this level. If he gets the job done, if he perseveres to his goal, then we can say he did not fall to the temptation of bribery or fail out of fear.

But the Op has identified himself with the forces of honesty: "If you've got a fairly honest piece of work to be done in my line, and you want to pay a decent price, maybe I'll take it on."[26] Honest—or fairly honest—work for an honest price is part of his code, so we have legitimate right to look at his behavior from a moral perspective.

But how honest can an honest man stay in a world of dishonesty and deception? Perhaps only "fairly honest," perhaps not at all. The Elizabethan and Jacobean revenge plays are striking examples of just such a problem; protagonists who, in the beginning, have a justifiable complaint and who possess moral awareness, find that as soon as they enter their corrupt worlds to pursue justice they must use the corrupt means of these worlds to survive. To employ corrupt means to attain moral ends, however, can have terrible consequences, as it does in *The Revenger's Tragedy*. By the end of the play, Vindice has lost all moral perspective and is seen, both by the readers of the play and by the good forces which come in at the end, as immoral and vicious as those whom he had hoped to defeat. This dilemma occurs repeatedly in such plays as *The Spanish Tragedy* and *The Revenger's Tragedy*, and through the first four acts of *Hamlet*. It is not until Hamlet's sea voyage and his confrontation with the gravedigger in Act Five that Hamlet comes to a new perspective, a new way of seeing his relationship to the world around him. He stops trying to shape events—the methods of the villains in the play—and realizes instead that

> "There's a divinity that shapes our ends,
> Rough-hew them how we will—"[27]

Hamlet has experienced life's unpredictability; he has come to accept its uncertainty. In one view of the play, Hamlet's madness has been partly the madness of trying to control events, trying to use the corrupt means of his world to accomplish moral ends.

Red Harvest resembles a revenge play in that the protagonist swears revenge, operates in a corrupt world, and even more significantly, chooses to use the very means of his enemies: Machiavellian policy. Initially it seems he has no other choice. He surely cannot be successful if he tries to fight all the corrupt powers in Poisonville by himself; he must, if he is to survive, use strategy, set one group against another, and stay clear of the ensuing bloodshed if possible. But whether he can avoid a similar fate to Vindice's or Hieronimo's is problematic. I intend to show, in fact, that to some degree he does not. Though he accomplishes his goal of cleaning up Personville, he becomes in the process a very ambiguous figure, belonging neither to the world of law and justice nor to the criminal world.

Like Hamlet or Vindice, the Continental Op sees very early in the novel that Machiavellian machination is the most effective and efficacious method of dealing with the multiple criminal elements. As early as Chapter Nine, the Op awakens "with an idea," a program for setting one group of gangsters against another. Specifically, having been told by Max Thaler that the Kid Cooper-Ike Bush fight was fixed for the sixth round, the Op begins to circulate that rumor, thus drastically altering the odds on the fight. At the same time, he uses the ex-cop MacSwain's greed to pry from him information about Ike Bush's past. As it turns out, Bush is really Al Kennedy, a former bank robber from Philadelphia. Using this information, the Op puts the squeeze on him: ". . . if Ike Bush doesn't turn in a win tonight, Al Kennedy will be riding east in the morning."[28]

The Op's blackmail squeeze is clear: Bush can go against the gamblers or he can go to jail. Moments before the fight begins, the Op informs Dinah Brand and her consumptive friend, Dan Rolff, that they must switch their bets from Cooper to Bush. The result is devastatingly effective. Ike Bush wins, thus making Thaler and the other gamblers lose heavily; and for winning because he had to, Ike Bush dies with a knife in his back. The only money winners are Dinah and Rolff, and this makes Thaler believe he had been sold out by Dinah: "This isn't the first time you've sold me out. It's the last." [29]

Her answer, "To hell, my love, with you!" accomplishes what the Op hoped for: a splitting of forces. Dinah splits with Thaler and joins the Op because she thinks he has the Midas touch.

Thaler is put in a suspicious position *vis a vis* his gambling partners. As Dinah puts it:

> "What's the matter with Max is he's afraid the others will think he was in on it too, that Dan was putting his dough down as well as mine. Well that's his hard luck. He can go climb trees for all I care, the lousy little runt."[30]

The Op's description of his own method is very enlightening:

> "That was only an experiment—just to see what would
> happen.... Plans are all right sometimes... and some-
> times just stirring things up is all right—if you're tough
> enough to survive, and keep your eyes open so you'll
> see what you want when it comes to the top."[31]

Stirring things up and trying to stay tough enough to survive
prove to be the Op's method throughout *Red Harvest*. In this
initial case, his method is tried out: it's a pragmatic experi-
ment, one which gets results even though a man is killed in the
process. It works because the Op has accurately evaluated the
passions and weaknesses of his antagonists. Because they are
either guilty of past corruption (Ike Bush) or greedy (MacSwain,
Dinah, Thaler, et al.) they unknowingly work against their own
interests and are helpless to avoid the concatenation of cause
and effect that the Op sets in motion. Unlike our feeling of
horror in *The Revenger's Tragedy* when we see Vindice kill the
Duke, here we are not morally upset that Ike Bush gets killed.
He is not innocent, and his death is seen, though as non-legal,
as poetic justice.

[50]

If one of the basic elements of the Op's code is to do what
he says he will do, then results are a major criteria for success.
As he defines it, results can cover messy details:

> "If it works out the way I want it to, I won't have to
> report all the distressing details... It's right enough for
> the Agency to have rules and regulations, but when
> you're out on a job you've got to do it the best way you
> can. And anybody that brings any ethics to Poisonville
> is going to get them all rusty. A report is no place for
> the dirty details..."[32]

Even realizing that the "distressing details" are human lives, we are not terribly disturbed at this amoral declaration, although it does cast ambiguity over what the Op must have meant when he talked earlier in the novel about "a fairly honest piece of work."

Personville does indeed seem to be a world devoid of values. The only moral spokesman in the novel is Dan Rolff (who physically resembles Hammett, and is tubercular as Hammett was himself), and he is suggestively diseased and impotent. His moral outburst at Dinah for being so willing to betray her former friends for money—"I said to betray your friends to this chap would be utterly filthy, and it would"[33]—earns him a terrific beating from Dinah. The only other moral protest is heard from Dick Foley, one of the Op's detective colleagues who quits the job because he suspects the Op has committed murder. But we see this, too, as an impotent protest. First of all it suggests that the only other possible alternative to the Op's methods is to leave town—hardly a tenable alternative when Poisonville still reeks with corruption.

But more importantly, one must see the inclusion of the Foley episode in the novel as an attempt by Hammett to sharpen our sense of his protagonist's strength of character and to complicate our moral evaluations of his actions. Though Foley's desertion might initially seem to be an artistic ploy to persuade us of the Op's growing corruptness, it is more likely that it is just the reverse. Foley's action reveals his faithlessness. He has an inadequate understanding of the Op and an equally inadequate understanding of the special nature of the Personville-Poisonville world and of the job at hand. His response to this ambiguous world, a response reflecting greater weakness than strength, contrasts to the Op's decision to stay and do what he can, and thus we feel a greater sympathy for the Op's very difficult position. As the Op puts it to Foley, "Go back to San

[51]

Francisco, Dick. I've got enough to do without having to watch you."[34]

Supporting evidence for such a reading is to be found in Mickey Linehan's decision not to leave the job. When the Op gives him the same chance he gave Foley, Mickey responds:

> "Don't get so cocky over one lousy murder that maybe didn't happen. But what the hell? You know you didn't lift her dough and pretties."[35]

Mickey's greater faith in his colleague and his keener sense of the reality of the situation—*i.e.*, that maybe it didn't happen— tends to lessen our approval of Foley's position. It is clear that Hammett's handling of the Foley-Linehan decisions should be seen as a representation technique to increase our identification with the Op, not as an attempt to criticize him.

Rules and regulations do seem somehow beyond the point in a world like *Red Harvest*, yet it is important that Hammett keeps reminding us indirectly that such things do exist. The outside world is not wholly forgotten; Personville may indeed be an unweeded garden, but we are occasionally reminded that another world lies outside. The minor events like Rolff's moral outbursts, the exit of Foley for what he implies are moral reasons, and the periodic references to the Old Man and the Continental Detective Agency by themselves do not mean very much, but together they operate to complicate our moral reflections to the Op. Hammett's use of the Old Man, for example, clarifies considerably the Op's dilemma in Poisonville. The Op's description of his boss is revealing:

> He was also known as Pontius Pilate, because he smiled pleasantly when he sent us out to be crucified on suicidal jobs. He was a gentle, polite, elderly person with

no more warmth in him than a hangman's rope. The Agency wits said he could spit icicles in July.[36]

Though a cold man, the boss is nevertheless a man of rules and regulations, a fact that bleakly contrasts to the Op's mode of behavior in the novel. But how are we to react to this contrast? To be sure, we are reminded that society expects its enforcers of the law to follow rules of conduct, but we have also experienced the world of Poisonville, a world where no values or ethics find expression. The reader is encouraged to see the startling difference between what ought to be and what is. Hammett keeps the Old Man outside Poisonville, and the Op inside. The stress seems to be on the difference between being within the world of corruption and being outside it. Inside Poisonville the Op experiences the clash between rules and legal procedures and the necessity of taking pragmatic action in a completely diseased world. He is on the firing line, not back in a cool, refined office. His dilemma is that he must act as he does, and yet feel the horror of this necessity.

Hammett even further deepens the problem of moral vision by showing the Op growing increasingly self-critical. The minor criticisms suggested by Rolff and Foley mirror his own ambivalence concerning his methods. At one moment he can see his method as precisely the right one:

> "I've got to have a wedge that can be put between Pete and Yard, Yard and Noonan, Pete and Noonan, Pete and Thaler, or Yard and Thaler. If we can smash things enough—break the combinations—they'll have their knives in each others backs, doing our work for us."[37]

This is sound Machiavellian policy: set up the right conditions and your enemies will exterminate themselves. Yet at another

[53]

moment Op will describe his method in such a way that we sense he sees real problems with it:

> "I could buy more dope on the whole lot from Dinah Brand. But there's no use taking anybody into court, no matter what you've got on them. They own the courts, and, besides, *the courts are too slow for us now.* I've got myself *tangled* up in something and as soon as the Old Man smells it—and San Francisco isn't far enough away to fool his nose—he's going to be sitting on the wire, asking for explanations. I've got to have *results* to hide the details under. So evidence won't do. What we've got to have is dynamite."[38]

He feels trapped, entangled by the Poisonville world. He is clearly uneasy with himself; the details of his job, he knows, will not bear the light of legal and moral scrutiny. He now needs dynamite, he implies, because he has established a tempo, a pace by which to order his plots and counterplots, and things are moving so quickly—and are apt to move even more quickly if his machinations are discovered—that legal means, even if possible, must now be ignored for survival's sake. He also knows that without results he is lost, as far as his boss is concerned, but that with results, the means will not be closely examined.

But the interesting moral question is: Could the Op have avoided such an entanglement? Hammett's choice of diction suggests that he could not. The courts are controlled by the corrupt powers, we are told, and they "are too slow for us now," a phrase that suggests that it is not just the Op's view that courts are too slow in general but that they are not efficacious for his present situation. The established allegorical typography makes it very clear that a detective representing the law and justice has a dilemma when the law itself is out of office. He must act without the usual supports of other police and the courts; he is left entirely on his own. Having a job to do, and in a world in which none of the convenient props exist, the Op must take the most pragmatic line. A reader agrees, finally, I think, that dynamite is more efficacious than evidence in this particular world at this particular time.

Robert Edenbaum describes Hammett's tough guys as daemonic, "free of sentiment, or fear of death" and what Albert Camus called "a man without memory," free of the burden of his past actions.[39] Such a comment seems to me to miss the point considerably. For example, the Op says

> Poisonville was beginning to boil out under the lid, and
> I felt so much like a native that even the memory of my
> very un-nice part in the boiling didn't keep me from
> getting twelve solid end-to-end hours of sleep.[40]

When he says this, we notice his toughness and resiliency, but we also notice that he does not deny possessing unpleasant memories; he is self-conscious, aware that the town is influencing him. He feels he has an affinity with it; he feels he is being pulled in by its poisonous quality, and Hammett shows us that this feeling increases in intensity as the Op becomes more deeply involved in Poisonville. Edenbaum would have us read such a declaration as lack of sentiment, but isn't the point rather that these lines show the quality of the Op's awareness? Though he can still sleep he feels tainted by the world around him.

The episodic nature of *Red Harvest* allows Hammett to portray the various plots of the Continental Op and their individual results. Unity of effect is achieved by having all the violent mayhem in the novel be the result of the Op's psychological game of chess. He drives a wedge between Noonan and Thaler which results in a bloody shoot-out at Cedar Hill

(Chapter Fifteen), and by Chapter Eighteen, Chief Noonan is broken by the pressure:

> "I'm getting sick of this killing. It's getting to me—on my nerves, I mean...Everybody's killing everybody. Where's it going to end?...I can't go through with it...I'm sick of this butchering."[41]

Noonan is crumbling, and he doesn't get our sympathy. As the one who represents the law's delay and the insolence of office, his breakdown is poetic justice. By contrast, the Op stands coolly by, confident that he can do what Noonan cannot: finish what he started. The Op uses Noonan's weakness to set up what becomes the climactic plot: "Tell them how you feel about it. Have a get-together and make peace."[42]

The Op's "peace conference" is at the same time the most perfect example of Machiavellian policy in the novel and the most revealing about the Op himself. The conference is a gathering of all the corrupt powers in Personville—Elihu Willsson, Pete the Finn, Reno Starkey, Max Thaler, Noonan—and the Op. All the parties are deceived in one way or another; only the Op knows the truth, and he chooses when to use it and when to distort it. For instance, Noonan thinks Max Thaler killed his brother Tim, and though the Op knows Noonan is deceived (because he deceived him!), he plays it as if Noonan has known all along that MacSwain really killed his brother and that he only pretended to think Thaler guilty so he might doublecross him. The Op has doublecrossed Noonan, and he describes Noonan's response: "He stared at me with dumbfounded eyes. He gaped. He couldn't understand what I had done to him."[43]

Elsewhere, the Op uses truth, but only if it will fire the passions of the villains. The Op knows he is in a good spot if he plays his hand right, and as he repeatedly sets the participants against each other, he can barely suppress laughter: "I pushed my lips together to keep from laughing at the panic in his voice."[44] The upshot of the Op's work is total enmity, not peace. The immediate result is Noonan's violent death only hours later by gunshots out of the dark.

Most interesting, however, is the Op's reaction to his own plan:

> "This damn burg's getting me. If I don't get away soon I'll be going blood-simple like the natives. There's been what? A dozen and a half murders since I've been here . . . I've arranged a killing or two in my time, when they were necessary. But this is the first time I've ever got the fever. It's this damned burg. You can't go straight here . . . How could I help it if the best way was bound to lead to a lot of killing? The job couldn't be handled any other way without Elihu's backing. . . . Play with murder enough and its gets you one of two ways. It makes you sick or you get to like it."[45]

What earlier could be slept off cannot be so easily handled now. The action has proliferated and pulled the Op into it. He feels corrupted by the society, but he defends himself by arguing that the *job* necessitated immoral action. There is, he implies, the job and morality, and the two cannot work together—at least in Poisonville. As he sees it, his role demanded that he act as he did: "So everybody sat around and behaved and watched everybody else while I juggled death and destruction."[46] Rather than seeing the Op as some demonic tough guy, I think Hammett intends us to see just how vulnerable he is. Hammett holds a delicate balance between the situation in Poisonville as the allegory represents it, and the situation the Op creates when he begins to work within that world. We do not doubt for a moment

[57]

the horrible moral or ethical position of the Op, either as it would be seen by those not of Poisonville, or as it is perceived by the Op himself, a man from the outside trapped inside.

But the question is, where does responsibility lie? The fable of Personville-Poisonville creates the situation in which a pragmatist is set against an extravagantly corrupt world. The Poisonville world is even more thoroughly lost in disease than Vindice's Italy in *The Revenger's Tragedy.* At least in that world a few good people do exist (Castiza, for one), and the thunder and the blazing star at the end of the play suggest the presence of a divine order still viable behind the darkness of the present disorder. The Op has vowed to clean up a community, to act as scourge, and we approve. Yet to accomplish the job he has had to employ the corrupt means of that world. In so doing, he has become soiled in the working, but we feel that this is inevitable. When he says, "How could I help it...?" the reader has no more of an answer than he does.

We sympathize with the Op because he is so very aware of his dilemma. We tend to agree that he did what he had to do. The novel renders in rather poignant terms and with some complexity the American myth of the rugged individualist who finds his identity in doing what he must do.

[58]

And yet the Op himself cannot be so easily satisfied. When Dinah Brand says to him, "It's not your fault, darling. You said yourself that there was nothing else you could do,"[47] Hammett has the Op reply:

> "There was plenty else I could do...I could have gone to him this afternoon and showed him that I had them ruined. *He'd have listened to reason.* He'd have come over to my side, have given me the support I needed to swing the play *legally.* I could have done that. But it was *easier* to have them killed off, easier and surer, and, now

that I'm feeling this way, more satisfying. . . Poisonville is right. It's *poisoned* me. . . Look. I sat at Willsson's table tonight and *played* them like you'd play trout, and got just as much *fun* out of it. I looked at Noonan and knew he hadn't a chance in a thousand of living another day because of what I had done to him, and I laughed, and felt warm and happy inside. That's not me. I've got hard skin all over what's left of my soul, and after twenty years of messing around with crime I can look at any sort of murder without seeing anything in it but my bread and butter, the day's work. But this getting a roar out of planning deaths is not *natural* to me. It's what this place has done to me."[48]

I quote at length because this is one of the few times that Hammett allows us to get behind the Op's stoical mask and to see within, and what we see is pain. On the one hand, there is Hammett's quasi-Marxian suggestion that society has alienated the worker from his profession. According to Kenneth Keniston's analysis of Karl Marx's concept of alienation, being at odds with one's work leads almost necessarily to alienation from self, what he calls self-estrangement.[49] In the above lines, the Op feels that the natural connection between him and his work has been poisoned by the materialistic society of Personville. As a result, he now feels a stranger to himself, one whose conscious self has somehow been forced to disassociate from his real self.

But equally interesting as this oft-repeated Marxian emphasis on the corruptive influence of society is the Op's personal recognition—and perhaps ours—that there were alternatives he could have taken despite the outside influence. Legal alternatives did in fact exist. The words which are most disturbing are "easier," "played," and "fun". We first saw such words in Chapter Seven where, by the Op's own phraseology, we are led to see the slight alteration in his motive for taking Elihu's offer to clean up Poisonville. The job ethic was there, but so was the personal revenge element: "Now I'm going to have my fun. I've got ten thousand dollars of your money to play with."[50]

Has the personal element really so distorted the Op's view that he has purposely overlooked other alternatives? He says so; he condemns himself, but how valid do we feel his estimate of himself is? How justified is his self-castigation? Hammett has so defined and structured our conception of the demonic world of Personville that the Op's actions have seemed somehow appropriate and inescapable, however disturbing. We feel with the Op the horror of his joy in setting up deaths, but we know that none of his plans would have worked had the others not been so greedy, so corrupt, and so vicious. Furthermore, as for those other alternatives he speaks of: What are they? At no time in the novel is old Willsson shown to have the potential of reasonableness, so how certain can we be that the Op's description of his probable behavior is accurate? Not very. Any other possible alternatives, such as the courts, we can only think would be at best half-way measures.

I would argue that Hammett's stress here is as equally on the problematic nature of the Op's judgments as on his morally diseased mind. Hammett shows how difficult judgment is. Is it that the Op is actually as immoral as his enemies, or is it that he feels threatened by the possibility of such degeneration? Though ambiguous, the bulk of the evidence would suggest the latter. Were he as "blood-simple" as he feels himself becoming, he would not be troubled by the threat of such a transformation. As it is, Hammett shows us the Op turning for psychic relief to Rolff's laudanum—his doped gin:

> Time went by as we drank and talked in a world that was rosy, cheerful, and full of fellowship and peace of earth.[51]

We sympathize with him because his action reflects a desperate desire to escape to a better world, a world where, in fact, peace and fellowship could exist.

The Op's mind threatens to become as diseased in Poisonville as Dan Rolff's body. This analogy, suggested by the Op's indulgence in the laudanum, is strengthened by Hammett's description of the detective's two dreams. Drugged, the Op's dreams mirror the extent to which his mind has become infected by his mission and his environment. The first concerns his relationship with a woman in a veil who, though he is sure he knows her well, is a stranger to him. Though she speaks to him, he cannot hear. She leaves and runs away, shouting "Fire! Fire!" as she chases fire engines up the street. At that moment he recognizes her but is unable to catch up with her. He spends the rest of his time searching for her, from Baltimore and Denver to Cleveland, Dallas, Boston, Louisville, New York, Jacksonville, El Paso, Detroit. He fails in his search. Tired and defeated, he ends up in a hotel lobby in North Carolina. Then the woman arrives and kisses him, as people in the station laugh.

This dream most clearly suggests the futility of the Op's actions. He appears alienated from humanity and cut off from a meaningful relationship with a woman. Only she is able to accomplish anything; she finds him. When she kisses him he is embarrassed. His impotency again reminds us of Dan Rolff's inability to handle Dinah, and Op's lack of reaction to her embrace seems consistent with his general inability to react on a basic human level to the people around him. He failed to pursue the more "human" alternative with Elihu earlier, and yet we felt that such an alternative was an impotent one; and here, as there, he is more concerned with his role (how he appears) than in being. The dream mirrors the futility and alienation that he has just articulated.

The second dream more clearly reflects the Op's inner chaos, pain, and fear. Significantly, the dream is about revenge.

Again he is in a strange city, this time hunting a man down on a Sunday morning with a knife. The hunted man laughs at the Op's efforts to capture him and laughs while the Op tramples on people's heads as he runs:

> Keeping one hand on the open knife in my pocket, I ran toward the little brown man, running on the heads and shoulders of the people in the plaza.[52]

Finally he reaches his victim:

> Squeezing his head in my one hand, I tried to bring the knife out of my pocket with the other—and realized that I had gone off the edge of the roof with him. We dropped giddily down toward the millions of upturned faces in the plaza, miles below.[53]

Revenger and victim go over together to their deaths—an appropriate analog to the situation in the novel at this point. From one perspective, the Op and the "little brown man" are one and the same. Such a reading could suggest that the Op is killing himself through his own actions.

Put another way, this dream reveals the Op's inner fear that he is "blood-simple," degenerating in the very process of taking pragmatic action. As the dream intimates, the pragmatic necessity of capturing the man leads to his own death. Seen from this perspective, the dream represents the Op's subconscious rejection of his conscious life. The separation he felt earlier between what the job ought to have been and what it has become here finds expression in a most terrifying portrait of self-estrangement.

Awakening, the Op finds the violence of his dreams reflected in the scene around him. Dinah has been stabbed to death with an ice pick. The dream scene marks the last time

Hammett allows the reader a glimpse into the Op's mind, and he does not show the Op as being changed either by his dreams or his earlier feelings that he was becoming corrupt. His self-analysis and confessional are not shown, in other words, to have any effect on his actions. He returns to his deadpan, stoical masks and efficiently continues to set up red harvests: the wholesale slaughter in Whiskeytown, Reno Starkey's strangling of Whisper Thaler, Rolff's shooting of Thaler and Reno, and his own separation from his client, Elihu, and the ducking out of town to avoid the consequences. The Op's dreams do not in any way make him more vulnerable to his enemies; he does not weaken. But the dreams do give us a momentary glimpse into his own horrified soul, and we sympathize with his feelings while admiring his strength in not yielding.

Hammett returns to letting the action speak for itself. With the death of Dinah and the Op under suspicion for her murder, a warrant is issued for his arrest. He is forced to go underground by adopting an alias. In the public's eye he is a criminal-at-large and the charge is believable enough to Dick Foley that he quits working with the Op and leaves town. Even the Op himself is not sure he isn't guilty, a doubt that forces him to walk, "keeping to the darker side of the darkest streets." He quotes Noonan's dictum, "What's got to be done has got to be done," [54] a line which may suggest the close affinity the pragmatic and committed detective has with corruption. For him to be successful, the detective must be able to think like the corrupt man, in this case even act like him, and this is necessarily an ambiguous position. But we make a moral distinction between the two in terms of ends: the Op's purpose is to clean up a community, not to perpetuate his own self-interest.

Hammett's portrayal of his protagonist as a hunted man in the last few chapters indicates his recognition of the dilemma of the moral and ethical pragmatist in a fallen world. We are shown that the Op is partially responsible for Dinah's death. Reno Starkey describes her death to him in this way:

> "You're hopped and she wants protection against Whisper coming back...You gallop out, coked to the edges, charging at the whole world with both eyes shut. She tumbles into you. You go down, roll around till your hand hits the butt of the pick. Holding on to that, you go sleep, peaceful as she is."[55]

Responsible for setting Reno and Whisper against each other, and Whisper against Dinah, the Op cannot protect her at the critical moment. Drugged, with his eyes shut, he is as impotent as he seems in his dreams,[56] and yet Dinah's complicity in the greed and corruption of Poisonville prevents any strong condemnation of the Op. We feel that her end is somehow an inescapable result of the way she has chosen to live.

Reno Starkey's death scene comments not only on Reno but the Op as well. Dying, Reno reminds us of the Op:

> He stopped, pretending interest in the shape the red puddle was taking. I knew pain had stopped him, but I knew he would go on talking as soon as he got himself in hand. He meant to die as he had lived, inside the same tough shell. Talking could be torture, but he wouldn't stop on that account, not while anybody was there to see him. He was Reno Starkey who could take anything the world had without batting an eye, and he would play it out that way to the end.[57]

Another hard-case like the Op, Reno will die as he lived. He has his own code and, like the Op, cannot or will not change. No one changes in *Red Harvest*; experience teaches nothing, and I think this is one of the fundamental points of the novel. Violence destroys violence, but there is little promise of regeneration. It is one of the central myths of America that violence can and does purge. As Richard Slotkin describes it:

> The myth of regeneration through violence defines one major component of the American mind, one stream of American consciousness, one major and characteristic conception of history and the cosmos held by Americans.[58]

Red Harvest is a novel of extreme violence, a megatomb of corpses, but what is the result of it all? The town is last seen under martial law, another kind of force, and though the Op has cleaned out a nest of corruption, there is no indication on Hammett's part that the purging is anything more than temporary.

Hammett emphasizes the Op's growing awareness of his own possible corruption up through Chapter Twenty-One, but does little with it from that point on. Possibly Hammett fails as a novelist here because he shuts off further exploration of the Op's character, but I argue that he has shown all that he needs to for his purposes. His refusal to go any further indicates in quite clear terms his vision of modern society and the dilemmas of the pragmatist in such a world. As long as the Op is committed to his moral intention to purge the Poisonville community, he is doomed to the shadowy world of pragmatic means. He must, as William F. Nolan puts it,

> Stay tough. Never show your tears. Don't back down to anybody. Learn to take it. Then maybe, just *maybe* you can survive. Go soft and you're finished. Stay cold, detached, hard, outwardly emotionless—and you've got a chance.[59]

A good summary of the hardboiled hero's code, these lines suggest what must be given up as well as what retained. At the end, the Op is separated temporarily from his name and forced to duck out of town. He tells us that he

> . . .spent most of my week in Ogden trying to fix up my reports so they would not read as if I had broken as many Agency rules, state laws and human bones as I had.[60]

Back in the outside world, the normal world of rules and procedures, the Op must prevaricate; he cannot tell the Old Man how it was in Poisonville, but we know. Hammett has rendered for us the problematic vision, and our understanding must surely run deeper than the Old Man's, or anyone else's in the normal world.

Hammett does not draw didactic conclusions concerning his protagonist. Color the ending gray; it is neither a condemnation of the Op and his methods nor an unqualified approval. Like the town, the Op is blighted. It is hard to see how Poisonville will ever become "a sweet-smelling and thornless bed of roses"[61] or the Op a normal man living a normal life. In a world where characters are not changed by their perceptions, in a world where (according to Hammett's descriptions) there are no more forceful passions than greed and the desire for power, and in a world where the representatives of law and order are at best men like the Op, it is difficult to see much hope. William Kenney argues that Hammett's depiction of violence, "brilliantly rendered as it often is. . .fails to point to anything beyond itself."[62] But this is questionable. Harold Orel is closer to the truth of *Red Harvest* when he comments on Hammett's conception of the private eye's role in society:

> Hammett always believed that the society which hired the "private eye" to protect it lived by questionable values.[63]

This is more to the point. Though an extreme instance, *Red Harvest* does present a vision of society that has its own tough truthfulness. It is not a romantic vision; the hero an anti-hero, tainted and vulnerable to corruption like everyone else, moves through a fragmented landscape alone with his own vision of what ought to be, and the strength enough to pursue it.

The novel's chilling tone is consistent throughout, and its message oblique. *Red Harvest* may not possess, as Warner Berthoff would say, a "visionary force, a transforming authority"[64] that a great novel should, but it does have its own truthfulness: a culture based on greed and violence is nightmarish, capable of no real renovation. Characterization, theme, and imagery all carry this suggestion, with the hero/anti-hero being, perhaps, the best example of the devastation such as society can wreak on the best of its people. The Op is neither a Natty Bumpo nor a Satan, but an ambiguous hybrid. He is the best man in his world, but his success and commitment extract a terrible price: his human feeling and impulses have to be suppressed and mutilated. To act is to be engaged necessarily in deception and violence; not to act is to be guilty of maintaining the diseased status quo. Hammett shows us the necessity for moral violence, but intimates that its harvest must be necessarily blighted. Eric Bentley once remarked on violence and social change by saying that

> If violence has the last word, it *will* have been an error and an absurdity though there may be no one left to see the joke.[65]

Red Harvest does suggest that violence may be the only real midwife of social change in a self-centered, corrupt system, but it equally suggests that violence wreaks such havoc on the souls of it perpetrators that regeneration may, at best, be only a dream that can find expression in a bottle of laudanum.

The Dain Curse *was published July 19, 1929. A copy of an
unsigned first edition, first printing in very good plus to near
fine condition in a similar condition dust jacket would be worth
$30,000 to $40,000 today. As with any other important first
edition, a copy in truly fine condition would be worth more.*

CHAPTER FOUR

The Dain Curse: A New Direction

HAVING SHOWN US CORRUPTION on a large scale, Hammett, in his second novel, *The Dain Curse* (1929), narrows the range of vision and concentrates on one family—the Dains. He moves us from the violent, brutal, dark world of Personville—symbolically modern America—into an equally twisted and domestic world of lust and hatred. The lust for power was the central driving force in *Red Harvest*; here in *The Dain Curse* it is sexual lust. The stain in the Dain family—lust and hatred—and its terrible effect on Gabrielle Dain Leggett is Hammett's focus. He moves from an exploration of society as a whole to an analysis of one of its parts: the family unit. Though we might expect him to write a very similar novel to his first one, we find this in not at all the case.

Critics have generally shied away from detailed commentary on *The Dain Curse* and, of all the novels of Dashiell Hammett, it is the least known and least liked. William Nolan points out that like *Red Harvest, The Dain Curse* was first written as separate novelettes for Joseph T. Shaw's *Black Mask*, and he argues that it suffers in its adaptation to book form:

> That he could bring the story off at all is to his credit— and there are few writers who could have unified the narrative's disparate parts as well as he—yet to some extent one could agree with Hammett himself who later called it "a silly story." *The Dain Curse* marked a plateau, not an upward step, in his career.[1]

In reading the novel we have the feeling of a four-part structure, but one that fails eventually to convince us of its unity. As originally published, the story had a four-part sequence. In the novel form, the four original sections—"Black Lives," "The Hollow Temple," "Black Honeymoon," "Black Riddle"—are cut to three and retitled, with little appearance of increased cohesiveness.[2]

[70]

Nolan's view that the novel represents a plateau for Hammett needs some analysis and clarification. Structurally the novel is inferior to *Red Harvest*. Unity of effect is not as well achieved as in the first novel because we feel that the three sections are artificially imposed on the matter. Yet at the same time, *The Dain Curse* presents a more balanced vision of reality than its predecessor because it renders a wider choice of possibilities for action and human behavior, and the world it describes is more of a mixture of good and evil, each possessing its own power and authenticity. Both as an individual novel and as a part of a larger and developing moral vision, *The Dain Curse* deserves a more detailed and complete examination than it has hitherto received.

Ross Macdonald once described plot as being a "vehicle of meaning" and added that

> It should be as complex as contemporary life, but balanced enough to say true things about it. The surprise with which a detective novel concludes should set up tragic vibrations which run backward through the entire structure. Which means that the structure must be single, and *intended*.[3]

The Dain Curse is Hammett's weakest novel because it is confused. It is not of one piece, and I think the cause of its failure can in part be explained by Hammett's attempt to embody his peculiar vision in a traditional form. Of the five novels, this is most like the classic detective story in conception, and the problem Hammett runs into is that of trying to make a form that depends on symmetry and unity of time and place carry the burden of rendering reality as problematic and deceptive.[4] Therefore his structuring of the parts of the novel is determined not by a single intention but by a two-fold intention, and the novel suffers a lack of focus.

Before exploring this point, however, it would be useful to consider another kind of comment on *The Dain Curse* that confuses the issue rather than clarifies it. William Kenney argues that the book fails in its creation of psychological probability:

> The trouble is that "human action" is an unsatisfactory term to use in discussing the novel, for in working out his intricate plot, Hammett compromises the reality of the humans who are involved in it. Continually one

[71]

has the impression that the characters are entirely at the service of the plot.[5]

Kenney's statement carries its own implicit assumptions about what ought to be in Hammett's novel. By suggesting that the novel is deficient because plot dominates character, Kenney seems to insist that Hammett should have written a more psychological novel, one in which the reader would be allowed to explore the psychological make-up of the villain—Owen Fitzstephan—and of Gabrielle Leggett, the girl of tortured and maimed sensibilities. But this seems a strange argument from one who is writing about the traditional detective story. Most of the classical stories, from Edgar Allan Poe and Arthur Conan Doyle to Dorothy Sayers and Ellery Queen, put plot before character. As Jacques Barzun puts it: "detection rightly keeps character subordinate."[6] Kenney fails to see that the real problem of the novel is not a matter of the relationship between plot and character but between preparation and discovery.

Hammett structures *The Dain Curse* so that it initially *appears* that its world is totally dislocated and confusing. The novel is divided into three sections: "The Dains," "The Temple," and "Quesada." At the end of each section the Op appears to have completed his assigned task, but each time he is rehired. Similar to *Red Harvest*, he is pulled deeper and deeper into the action, but unlike the earlier novel, he is not pulled in by his own emotional involvement. He keeps his distance, and thus never loses perspective.

The Op's first job is to recover some diamonds stolen from Edgar Leggett; having found the diamonds, the Op is then rehired by Madison Andrews, the Leggett's family lawyer, to guard Gabrielle while she resides at the Temple of the Holy Grail (Part II); then with that job seemingly complete, he is hired by Eric Collinson, Gabrielle's new husband, but he is killed before the Op arrives in Quesada (Part III); finally the Op is hired by the Collinson family to discover the killer of their son (Part III).

The major events of the novel involve a variety of characters who, at first sight, appear to have little to do with one another. Each event, moreover, appears to be something other than it is. The Leggett diamond robbery turns out to be a phony, Edgar Leggett's suicide turns out to be murder, his confession is a tissue of manufactured lies, and Alice Dain Leggett's death, though it too appears to be an accident, is also murder. In Part Two, Gabrielle goes to the Temple of the Holy Grail for rest and psychic recovery from having lost a mother, a father, and for having become addicted to drugs. But instead of recovery, she finds herself enmeshed in a twisted cult that sustains itself on drugs, mirages, and prestidigitation. In Part Three, hired by Eric Collinson, the Op comes to Quesada only to find that Eric has been killed. It first appears to be accidental; later it turns out to be murder. Mrs. Cotton's letter, written supposedly just before she is killed by Harvey Whidden, also turns out to be a sham. Next Whidden is killed while apparently resisting arrest, an action that covers his real intention of trying to kill Owen Fitzstephan. Then Fitzstephan is shattered by a bomb that "accidentally" explodes in his hand; and, finally, Gabrielle's "confession" turns out to be as phony as Mrs. Cotton's or Edgar Leggett's back in Part One. Hers is merely a hysterical reaction, a withdrawal symptom from morphine.

[73]

These actions all turn out to be other than they seem. In the last two chapters we discover that Owen Fitzstephan is responsible for all that has happened. Chapter Twenty-Two and Twenty-Three serve as the discovery scenes, and the confusion in the novel gives way to clarity. Fitzstephan's motive all along has been his lustful desire to possess Gabrielle, not out of love but egoism. More generally, he has an obsession to influence people in obscure ways. As a novelist, he has failed to influence, so he established the cult in the Temple. We are told that Leggett's robbery was Fitzstephan's idea: "...he didn't care what happened to her so long as he could ruin Leggett and get Gabrielle."[7] He was also responsible for the murders of Alice and Edgar Leggett, Doctor Riese, Eric Collinson, Mrs. Cotton, and Whidden.

Hammett's structural key is to have the three parts held together by a single cause, Fitzstephan, but to delay our recognition of this fact until the very end. Such an intention is very traditional, practically imitating one of the cardinal rules of the classical genre: "If the end is not to be a wordy anticlimax, some provocation of sharp surprise must be kept to the last."[8] But he mishandles the preparation sections by leaving almost *all* the explication till the end. So much weight is placed on the discovery scenes that the satisfying feeling that should arise from seeing order come from disorder is marred by our irritation that somewhere the progressive reasoning steps of the Op have eluded us. The denouement is satisfactory in the sense that the revelations make perfect sense of what has gone before, but Hammett has not so handled his detective in the earlier scenes that we are prepared for his leap to this conclusion at this particular time.

If we look at the preparatory scenes carefully, for example, it appears as if Hammett tried to avoid just such a mistake. At the end of each of the first two parts the Op and Fitzstephan meet and engage in an analysis of the foregoing action. Evident in these discussions are several indications that the Op begins to see problems with Fitzstephan's interpretation of events. Simultaneously, the reader comes increasingly to see that Fitzstephan is an egomaniac and capable of imaginative, even artistic, distortion. Though Hammett establishes probability for Fitzstephan's doing what he does, he fails to allow the Op to come to any explicit understanding of any one of the mysteries before the final two chapters. Then he presents the reader with an extremely complex explication of the previous action. It is simply too much.

Raymond Chandler once commented that a good mystery story must possess simplicity of structure: the "ideal denouement is the one in which everything is made clear in a brief flash of action."[9] Though Hammett plants behavioral clues throughout the novel,[10] he fails to focus on the Op's gradual movement towards clarity. Both the rendering of the problematic nature of reality and an orderly, sequential movement toward the denouement could have been achieved had Hammett allowed the reader to move step by step with the Op's growing sense that underlying the seemingly diffuse action there lay a pattern, perhaps designed by his friend Fitzstephan. Total clarity would still be left to the last, the moment the Op learns that Fitzstephan had loved Gabrielle, but there would be a greater harmony between preparation and discovery than presently exists.

In fact, examination of the opening sections of the novel suggest Hammett may have had just such a strategy in mind. In our first meeting with Fitzstephan we are told by the Op:

> I had met him five years before, in New York, where I was digging dirt on a chain of fake mediums who had taken a coal-and-ice dealer's widow for a hundred thousand dollars. Fitzstephan was plowing the same field for literary material. We became acquainted and pooled forces. I got more out of the combination than he did, since he knew the spook racket inside and out. . .[11]

From these lines we know that the Op has experienced fake mediums before—helpful experience in tracking down the fake ones of this novel, Fitzstephan and his curse—and that

[75]

Fitzstephan knows the spook racket thoroughly. This sets up the probability for what we learn later, namely that he is the mastermind behind the creation of the phony Temple of the Holy Grail.

Throughout these early chapters Hammett enforces the probability that Fitzstephan possesses the qualities of a villain, though it is quite subtle. For example, he makes repeated use of such *double entendres* as the following:

> Fitzstephan said: "I suppose you're still hounding the unfortunate evil-doer?"
>
> "Yeah. That's how I happened to locate you. Halstead tells me you know Edgar Leggett."[12]

On first reading, such innocuous comments pass over us, but on second reading they take on more pointed resonances. Fitzstephan's following comment to the Op, though humorously put, indicates an important trait in his character:

> "Don't try to be subtle with me, my son; that's not your style at all. Try it and you're sunk."[13]

[76] As the novel develops, Hammett increasingly paints in sharper and sharper terms Fitzstephan's ego and his denigration of the Op's abilities. Consider these three examples:

- "Always belittling," he said. "You need more beer to expand your soul."
- "But come, my boy. I'm listening. Let's have the story, and then I can tell you where you erred."
- "You're stumped, bewildered, flabbergasted. Do you admit you've met your master, have run into a criminal too wily for you?"[14]

On a second reading, these lines rightly suggest Fitzstephan's egoistic notion that he is a demonic artist weaving such a rich tapestry of criminality that common people, like the Op, have no chance to perceive its subtleties.

Hammett conjoins this stress on Fitzstephan's almost maniacal egoism with an equal stress on the Op's growing perception that the seemingly incoherent events are somehow coherent at bottom. Fitzstephan consistently derides the Op's arguments that the curse cannot explain the events, but the Op persists:

> "But the trouble with it is it's worked out too well, too regularly. It's the first one I ever ran across that did."[15]

Later he says, concerning the things that have befallen Gabrielle:

> "Her father, step-mother, physician, and husband have been killed, one after the other, in less than two months; and her maid jailed for murder. All the people closest to her. Doesn't that look like a program?"[16]

After listing all the murders and killings and disappearances, the Op remarks to Fitzstephan:

> "Call any couple of pairs coincidences. You'll still have enough left to point at somebody who's got a system he likes, and sticks to it."[17]

Taking all these references, and putting them along side of the fact that Hammett places Fitzstephan either on or near the scene of each murder or disappearance, it becomes clear that Hammett is creating the probabilities for what is later to be discovered. Why then deny the reader some involvement with the Op's analytical speculation? By Chapter Nineteen the Op knows the answers; he knows because Gabrielle tells him that Fitzstephan loved her. This is the motive that explains all that has happened, yet even here the Op does not reveal what he suspects. All he says to Gabrielle is,

> "I'm going to show you that your curse is a lot of hooey, but it'll take a few days, maybe a couple of weeks."[18]

Not letting the reader in on what he surmises accomplishes little. The reader cannot be far behind the Op's perceptions, and this unnecessary mystification adds nothing to the novel. In fact, it weakens the overall effect by needlessly demanding the crowding of all revelatory information in at the end and thus destroying the delicate balance that might have been achieved between mystification and knowledge.

Jacques Barzun tells us that the art of "half-concealment" is "an art which is none other than literary."[19] And Dorothy Sayers, commenting on the "fair play doctrine," says the difficult problem for a writer of a mystery story is, "How can we at the same time show the reader everything and yet legitimately obfuscate him as to its meaning?"[20] It is this problem that Hammett has not successfully solved.

[78] And it is a shame. It weakens one of the strongest themes of the novel, which is that reality is highly problematic. Hammett stresses throughout the difference between the Op's view of how to find truth and Owen Fitzstephan's. In one of their confrontations, the Op tells Fitzstephan:

> "You've got a flighty mind. That's no good in this business. You don't catch murderers by amusing yourself with interesting thoughts. You've got to sit down to all the facts you can get and turn them over and over till they click."[21]

His is basically a *gestalt* theory of reality; turn data over and over until the organizing principle is discovered. He recognizes that our perception of reality is imperfect because our minds are imperfect:

> "Nobody thinks clearly, no matter what they pretend. Thinking's a dizzy business, a matter of catching as many of those foggy glimpses as you can and fitting them together the best way you can. That's why people hang on so tight to their beliefs and opinions; because, compared to the haphazard way in which they're arrived at, even the goofiest opinion seems wonderfully clear, sane, and self-evident. And if you let it get sway from you, then you've got to dive back into that foggy muddle to wangle yourself out another to take its place."[22]

More philosophical than usual, the Op implies that we create fictions about ourselves in order to survive. This is one reason Fitzstephan's fiction about the Dain curse so entrances Gabrielle: it seems to account for what otherwise appears to be incoherent and insane. But the Op believes nothing is so perfect:

> "But that brings us to the human mind behind it—one that can bungle—and not your infallible curse."[23]

[79]

Although Fitzstephan tries to mislead Gabrielle and the Op into believing his romantically gothic view of reality, the Op knows better and looks for answers more akin to his conception of what reality is.

In short, Hammett implies that some answers are possible, although it takes a great deal of juggling of data and theory. In order to suggest the power of the intelligence, Hammett portrays the numerous discussions between Fitzstephan and the Op.

Placed strategically, these discussions are supposed to illustrate two differing views of reality, but unfortunately the conflict is not made as clear as it could or ought to be. Since clarity is to be reached eventually, there is no reason Hammett could not show one epistemology gradually coming to dominate the other as the novel draws to a close. Like Herman Melville in *Moby Dick*, Hammett raises the specter of inscrutable malice. His emphasis on life as perilous and overly subtle echoes Melville's description of the sea:

> Consider the subtleness of the sea; how its most dreaded creatures glide under water, unapparent for the most part, and treacherously hidden beneath the loveliest tints of azure.[24]

Ishmael's description of reality sounds very similar to the Op's:

> My dear sir, in this world it is not easy to settle these plain things. I have ever found your plain things the knottiest of all. And as for this whole spout, you might almost stand in it, and yet be undecided as to what it is precisely.[25]

Man can never know certainty, Melville implies in *Moby Dick*, and though Hammett plays with this concept he finally ends by intimating man can have partial knowledge. The inscrutable malice which afflicts Gabrielle and which involves the Continental Op is finally uncovered. Cause and effect links are established; full knowledge, it is implied, is either impossible to have—for example, how sane or insane is Fitzstephan?—or better left unexplored for humane reasons. This latter point is made by the Op who decides that it were better he not pursue the truth of Gabrielle's childhood actions. Did she actually kill her real mother, Lily Dain Leggett, as Alice Dain Leggett says (Chapter Seven) or can we believe Fitzstephan's declaration to the Op that Alice lies only in order to further revenge herself on Gabrielle (Chapter Twenty-Three)? Whatever the full truth (and we suspect the latter), the Op makes the moral decision that it is best left unexplored: "It was nobody's business except Gabrielle's, and she seemed happy enough with what had already been dug up."[26]

That the Op acts on the understanding that truth should be combined with feeling shows us how fundamentally different is the moral vision of this novel from that of *Red Harvest*. Melville's phrase, "oh, horrible vultureism of earth! from which not the mightiest whale is free,"[27] may be an apt epigraph for *Red Harvest* and the moral dilemma of its hero, but surely is too pessimistic for *The Dain Curse*. The world is corrupt enough, to be sure. The inefficiency and ambitiousness of District Attorney Vernon and Sheriff Feeney paint a bleak picture of the law as does the obvious corruption of the legal process by Marshall Dick Cotton, who attempts to frame his wife's sexual playmate for her murder (Chapter XVI). The minor plots of the novel—the Haldrons in the Temple of the Holy Grail and the law officers in the last part of the novel—mirror the underlying causes of the major plot. In the larger plot, Alice Dain Leggett twists Gabrielle's mind, presumably kills her sister Lily, and finally murders her husband Edgar out of diabolical lust and hatred, a madness that parallels Fitzstephan's. In both major and minor plots, sexual lust and hate pervert judgments and throw human relationships into chaos. In this respect, the vultureism of which Melville speaks finds adequate expression.

But this *Red Harvest* view of humanity is not the only one rendered. Though the novel is the weakest of the novels in form, it nevertheless reveals interesting things about Hammett as an artist. Hammett does very imaginative things in *The Dain Curse*, not the least of which is his handling of the hero and the villain. *Red Harvest* had no outstanding villain; everyone was tainted by the general malaise of corruption. The emphasis is decidedly on society first, and character second. The ambiguous hero Op in the first novel is pretty much a one-dimensional man, but in *The Dain Curse* Hammett splits this ambiguous figure into two distinct personalities. Though still conceived as an outsider, the Op is more the businesslike detective. He does not originate action in the novel and, though occasionally cynical and overly harsh, he is more temperate and human than in the first novel.[28] His Iago-like abilities of that novel are here given to Owen Fitzstephan who, as rendered by Hammett, is almost a blood-brother in technique, though not in motivation, to the early Op. His ability to make murder look like an accident, appearance like reality, self-interest like altruism, and ego like humility inescapably remind one of Shakespeare's Iago who, in *Othello*, could deceive everyone into believing that illusion was reality.

Though I do not wish to push the parallel too far, it is clear that the earlier Op's lust for revenge and blood is transformed into Fitzstephan's lust for Gabrielle Leggett. Both passions result in some form of mutilation to the possessor of those passions. The Op felt he suffered temporary "blood-simple" insanity, and Fitzstephan suffers more permanent physical mutilation and is found legally insane. Hammett further enforces this parallel by establishing that the Op and Fitzstephan are good friends throughout and rivals towards the end.

The purpose for this splitting of his earlier hero may suggest Hammett's own unease with this ambiguous creation, but it more probably reflects his interest in experimentation. In *Red Harvest* character is deemphasized, and the emphasis is on the force of social corruption. In this second novel, Hammett tries to do what proves an impossible task for him: to combine character analysis with classic detective mystification. The confusion of the novel stems from Hammett's obvious interest in suggesting the tortured psychology of Owen Fitzstephan and the emotionally torn Gabrielle and yet employing a form in which such revelation is prohibitive. The detective is necessary, both to solve the crimes and to start Gabrielle back on the path of sanity, but Hammett's real focus is on how vulnerable goodness is and how easily twisted the human mind can become if passion for the self rules. Though Hammett isn't able to master this attempt, he does establish a new pattern, a new possibility, for the detective story which is later taken up and explored more fully by Raymond Chandler and Ross Macdonald.

As in *Red Harvest,* deception is the unifying element of *The Dain Curse.* Though the novel is faulty in construction, Hammett gives the illusion of a greater unity than actually exists by the creation of an informing moral and social vision. In the first novel there seems to be no order beneath the deception, moral or otherwise, but in the second there is. Owen Fitzstephan is discovered to be the cause of evil, and the Op is the discoverer. There is a greater stability of vision in this novel because the Op's insight and intelligence make sense of the multiple layers of mystification and confusion. Further, as the events and their cause gradually become clear, values such as goodness and love for the first time in Hammett begin to have some strength of their own.

[83]

Hammett presents a more balanced view of human worth and potentiality in *The Dain Curse.* There are good people in the novel, people like the limited but well-intentioned Eric Collinson, his mother and father, and the worthy cop Detective Sergeant O'Gar. Gabrielle, battered and scarred, is adopted by the Collinsons:

She was in the Collinsons' hands now. They had come to Quesada for her as soon as the newspapers put out their first extra accusing Fitzstephan of Eric's murder...the Collinsons had simply seemed to pick her up, as was their right as her closest relations....[29]

She is regenerated not through violence but through love and devotion. She blooms under such influence: "...she came back to the city looking like nothing that she had been. The difference was not only in appearance."[30] Hammett suggests that though the world is perilous, fraught with contingencies such as heredity and environment, and further complicated by our inability to see clearly, there is yet the saving power of love and compassion.

Even Hammett's handling of his protagonist suggests such a balance. I have already argued that he draws back from further investigation into Gabrielle's past because he is aware that truth is best served with compassion, but it would be a mistake to see him as sentimental. From the outset he has been cool, business-like, and occasionally brutal. To search for truth in a world of violence and deception one must be tough and Hammett's Op is surely that. When, for example, Eric Collinson wants him to take Gabrielle to a hospital instead of to her home because she is coked on drugs, the Op refuses:

> "Her life's in no more danger than yours or mine. She's simply got a little more of the junk in her than she can stand up under. And she took it. I didn't give it to her."[31]

His realistic, take-your-consequences philosophy admits no sentimentality. He has a job to do, and he doesn't have time to administer balm to delicate egos like Eric's. Eric is shown to be completely helpless in time of crisis, and we admire the Op's ability to think and act quickly. Later in Chapter VII, his relentless pursuit of truth is evidenced in his merciless verbal hammering of Alice Leggett in front of Gabrielle. But it works: Alice confesses her past crimes and her hatred for Gabrielle before being killed in a scuffle with Fitzstephan. Eric again calls the Op brutal:

> Collinson, chafing the unconscious girl's hands, looked at me as if I were something there ought to be a law against, and said:
> "I hope you're satisfied with the way your work got done."
> "It got done," I said.[32]

The Op is a pro, all business. As he himself puts it, "I hadn't made such a mess of that first job: my efficiency offset my brutality..."[33]

We met this "ends justify the means" philosophy in *Red Harvest*, but here Hammett creates a world in which pragmatic action does not force the detective into inescapable moral dilemmas. Perhaps one of the reasons Hammett chose to use the traditional detective form was that it allowed him to remove his protagonist from the center of the action by making him a baffled but determined searcher for the truth, thus avoiding the moral and ethical pitfalls that threaten the Op in *Red Harvest*, in which he creates as much havoc and destruction as his enemies. Because he is not as influenced by the evil and corruption around him as his earlier prototype, he is not tempted to use his efficiency as a weapon of personal revenge. For example, at the end of Part Two, though he is interested in where the truth may be in the strange and violent episodes he has just witnessed in the Temple, he declines to pursue the matter further because the job he was hired for is technically over:

"There's a lot I'd like to do yet, but I was hired, this time, by Andrews, to guard her while she was in the Temple. She isn't there now . . ."[34]

Furthermore, pragmatic action in *The Dain Curse* is shown to be not merely necessary but conducive to moral health. The Op's tough—even brutal—behavior is shown to be a necessary condition of Gabrielle's recovery. She must, as it were, pass through the fiery crucible of his enforced cure before she can receive the balm of the Collinsons' compassion.

Hammett has created a good deal of sympathy for her psychological plight. She has been psychologically mutilated since childhood, having grown up hating her father and thinking him a murderer, losing her mother and gaining the twisted Alice as step-mother, turning to drugs for escape, having her husband murdered, and believing that she killed her mother and feeling she lives under a curse for it. Twice since childhood she has attempted suicide, and as the Op describes her, we see that she has had to carry Ophelia-like burdens totally alone:

> " . . . all the calamities known to man have been piled up on you, and your belief in your curse has made you hold yourself responsible for every item in the pile."[35]

But, as he also sees, she is " . . . too young, inexperienced, and self-centered to judge how she varied from the normal . . ."[36] She can be regenerated, but she must come back to life largely on her own. More self-pity won't help, and this is the job the Op takes in Chapters Twenty through Twenty-Two. Where earlier in the novel he would go no further than the hired job, here, because he is sensitive to her condition, he does.

He accomplishes his purpose through deception. He tells his partner Mickey Linehan that: "It's important that she keep on thinking I'm hot stuff." He builds Gabrielle's confidence by stressing to her that she possesses the inner strength of her father and that she can rely on him to aid her in her stated desire to kick the morphine habit. Yet nowhere does he become personally involved; he keeps his distance, more feigning sympathy than feeling it: "I made myself laugh as if I were sympathetic. . ."[37]

Gabrielle asks the Op: "Do I believe in you because you're sincere? Or because you've learned how—as a trick of your business—to make people believe in you?"

He observes: "She might have been crazy, but she wasn't stupid."[38]

Later, the Op does not indulge in sentiment when she grasps his hand and says,

"I'm going to believe you," she said. "I do believe you. I'm going to believe you no matter what you say."[39]

Hammett turns our own possible sentimental response aside by focusing on realistic details: "Her hands were clammy. I squeezed them and said: 'That'll be swell!'"[40] Following her night of hell—the withdrawal period—she asks him,

"Why did you go through all this with—for me?" She was really serious now.[41]

and he leads her to believe that he is very close to being in love with her:

"I'm twice your age, sister; an old man. I'm damned if I'll make a chump of myself by telling you why I did it, why it was neither revolting nor disgusting, why I'd do it again and be glad of the chance."[42]

His performance serves its purpose. Gabrielle tells us it was most efficacious in aiding her recovery:

> "I honestly believed you all afternoon—and it *did* help me. I believed you until you came in just now, and then I saw— . . .A monster. A nice one, an especially nice one to have around when you're in trouble, but a monster just the same, without any human foolishness like love in him . . ."[43]

The Op gives her what she needs most—confidence in herself—and his pretense of having fallen in love with her is (as is his allowing her to think that the two bags of sugar are dope) simply the most efficient way of solving her problem. Fitzstephan and Alice had destroyed her sense of herself by means of lies and deceptions, and the Op simply returns it using the same means.

Hammett does not allow romanticism to color realism. Detectives like Raymond Chandler's Philip Marlowe or Ross Macdonald's Lew Archer actually suffer with their clients, but Hammett's Op does not. Hammett implies that reality is not words, or even thoughts; rather, it is actions. Though the Op's words are misleading, his action is nevertheless a sensitive and humane one, and it is by this that we must judge him.

Lastly, *The Dain Curse* renders a view of justice quite different from that of *Red Harvest*. For one, the villains are not handled punitively. In the earlier novel Op vowed that no one would escape his sword of justice, but here he goes to court to proclaim that Fitzstephan "was legally entitled to escape hanging." Owen Fitzstephan convinced a jury that he was insane, and "A year later he was discharged. I don't suppose the asylum officials thought him cured: they thought he was too badly crippled ever to be dangerous again."[44] Poetic justice replaces punitive force.

In fact, one could argue that poetic justice exists in both novels, but the crucial difference is that in *The Dain Curse* the Op does not arrange the events and therefore avoids the charge of having played demi-god. Hammett shows us that Fitzstephan's defeat is totally his own doing. Like Claudius, Laertes, Rosencrantz, and Guildenstein in *Hamlet*, he is hoist by his own petard. As the Op tells us, Fitzstephan could not have avoided taking the packaged bomb that Tom Fink handed him:

> He couldn't have refused to take it without attracting my attention, without giving away the connection between him and Fink. He had concealed it until we had left the room, and then had opened it—to wake up in the hospital.[45]

Having lived a tissue of lies throughout, Fitzstephan is trapped, and cannot save himself. The bomb cripples him for life. Just as his body suffers appropriate mutilation, so his ego, the driving force behind his diabolic acts, suffers a similar fate. In the see-sawing battle of wits with the Op, he finally suffers defeat. At the end, he hates the Op not because the Op discovered his plot but because the Op will not accept Fitzstephan's argument that he is sane:

> This sudden hatred of me...had grown, I supposed, out of his knowing I thought him insane. He wanted the rest of the world...to think he had been crazy—and did make them think so—but he didn't want me to agree with them. As a sane man who, by pretending to be a lunatic, had done as he pleased and escaped punishment, he had a joke—if you wanted to call it that—on the world. But if he was a lunatic who,

ignorant of his craziness, thought he was pretending to be a lunatic, then the joke—if you wanted to call it that—was on him. And my having such a joke on him was more than his egoism could stomach . . .[46]

"There's a divinity that shapes our ends, Rough-hew them how we will—"

Such was Hamlet's conception of his world, and Fitzstephan, had he been able to see himself with clarity, might well have said much the same. Beneath the fog of our perceived existence, Hammett implies, lies such a mysterious order and intelligence, but as Fitzstephan's silence suggests he will never see it.

Like the villains in *Red Harvest*, the Op's range of possibilities for action were limited, but here Hammett shows a greater range of choices that an individual can make. Although death and degeneration exist and threaten, there is love and compassion as well. Regeneration is possible, though difficult. As Hammett presents it in the person of Gabrielle, regeneration doesn't just happen. It must be willed through great personal effort. Gabrielle must will to pass through the gauntlet of the Op's cure before she can find a home with the Collinsons. Hammett's point seems to be that in this world one makes one's own stability and freedom through action, like Gabrielle, or loses them, as Fitzstephan does.

In the end, Gabrielle's perseverance, the Collinsons' loyalty, and the Op's common sense triumph. The novel shows that life is cruel and uncertain, but not bereft of meaningful modes of action. The predominance of corrupt figures in *The Dain Curse* gives us the feeling that modern society is largely a moral wasteland, a society where people prey on others to feed their own sickness, be it greed, hate, or lust. The general implication is that people have forgotten how to be human. Fitzstephan's way of regarding Gabrielle is perhaps all too common. Regarding her as a precious object, his violent actions to possess her increase her economic value to him:

> He looked on Gabrielle now as his property, bought with the deaths he had caused. Each death had increased her price, her value to him.[47]

Hammett's diction suggests the Marxian view that the capitalistic system must eventually corrode from within. The extent of Fitzstephan's corruption is clarified when we discover that he is himself a Dain: his mother and Gabrielle's maternal grandfather were brother and sister, and therefore his earlier lust for Alice Dain, and his present lust for Gabrielle, is incestuous. It may be that Hammett chose to focus on the family unit—in particular the Dains—to suggest the Marxian view that corrosion of the human spirit in a materialistic society is both gradual and inevitable.

Such emphasis is clearly present in the novel, but it is balanced by the positive portraits of the Collinsons, Gabrielle, and the Op. Hammett's detective resembles what Maurice Friedman calls the "Modern Sisyphus," one who posits meaning and value *in spite* of the absurdity he sees around him.[48] *The Dain Curse* is a highly interesting and important work for what it tells us about Hammett's developing artistic talents and moral vision, but with its over-abundance of characters, its forced divisions, and its failure to prepare us adequately for the discovery scenes, it is not hard to see why Hammett would express his own disappointment by calling it "a silly story."[49] It is not what he wanted, but it is a step toward the technique and vision that he creates most satisfyingly in *The Maltese Falcon*.

The Maltese Falcon *was published on Valentine's Day, February 14, 1930. A copy of an unsigned first edition, first printing of a very good plus to near fine condition book in a similar condition dust jacket would be worth $80,000 to $100,000 today.*

CHAPTER FIVE

The Maltese Falcon:
The Emergence
of the Hero

D ASHIELL HAMMETT'S THIRD NOVEL, *The Maltese Falcon* (1930), has been called his best by most critics and for good reason. The development of character we noted as Hammett moved from his Op in *Red Harvest* to the one in *The Dain Curse* finds maturity in the creation of Sam Spade, the detective of *The Maltese Falcon*. As if to signify that a fully realized identity has come into being, Hammett for the first time gives his protagonist a name, and for the first time articulates a fully realized moral vision. Ambiguity exists, but despite what some interpreters have argued, there is no ambiguity in Spade's behavior at the end.

Few critics agree on how we should take the ending, but I will argue that the final confrontation between Sam Spade and Brigid O'Shaughnessy represents more clearly than any other in Hammett's writing the nature and scope of his moral vision. Spade's rejection of Brigid is at once pragmatic and moral, and it is a measure of Hammett's artistic development that he shows these to be interrelated and interdependent. In *Red Harvest* the pragmatic strain dominated, and the implication was that action in the real world had little or no functional relationship to moral concerns. *The Dain Curse* modified this view considerably, suggesting that moral action was possible, but Hammett did not allow his operative to become personally involved in the passions of the other characters. In *The Maltese Falcon* there is equally emphasis on the necessity of knowing the real world as it is (the pragmatic perception), and on acting according to principles (the moral code).

Such a reading, however, is clearly at odds with most of the critical estimates of the novel. We are told by one commentator, for example, that Spade is almost "totally amoral, almost cruel,"[1] and by another that Spade is simply one of Hammett's daemonic tough guys, "as amoral or immoral as his Antagonist."[2] Robert Edenbaum sees the novel as a battle between a "villain(ess) who is a woman of sentiment, and who thrives on the sentiment of others, and a hero who has none and who survives because he has none."[3] He would have us believe that Spade's "unscrupulousness" is the subject of the novel; he argues that Spade knows Brigid is guilty from the beginning and that he uses her and manipulates her throughout.[4] Irving Malin, on the other hand, sees Spade as an elusive and indefinable character, one who "shares the archetypal qualities of such mythical heroes as Odysseus, Samuel, and Jesus, and who yet seems to lack discernable motives for his actions."[5] Malin summarizes his position on *The Maltese Falcon* by saying:

Hammett is able to undercut traditional values of heroism, quest, and romance by disguising idealism as cynicism, prophecy as sham, serious play as "sport." He resembles Spade: Hammett too eludes us as we try to determine the underlying motives for his curious, new mythology.[6]

Walter Blair, however, offers a reading divergent from these views and much more sympathetic to my approach. He quotes Oscar Handlin's description of Hammett's characters—"Their virtues were distinctly personal—courage, dignity, and patience; and to them the hero clung for their own sake"[7]—and goes on to argue:

> Honor to Sam Spade was conformity to a code of rules which he himself invented, a means of demonstrating his own worth against the world.[8]

Blair concludes that by the end "Spade's actions make clear that he is the only character who has integrity, who obeys a code...Despite the fact that he has fallen in love with Brigid, he determines to turn her over to the police."[9]

More disparate views would be hard to come by. Where Blair and Handlin see Spade as a moral figure of courage, Grella sees him as cruel and immoral; Edenbaum agrees with Grella, and Malin plainly can't make up his mind. Perhaps William Kenney's statement on the novel may suggest some reasons for such variance of critical estimate. In saying that *The Maltese Falcon* is of major importance in the history and development of the modern detective novel, he says:

> Like Dorothy Sayers in her late novels, and Anthony Berkeley in the novels signed Francis Iles, Hammett

in *The Maltese Falcon* reduces the detective element to so minor a role that one hesitates to speak of it as a detective novel at all. It seems, rather, a novel about a detective, quite another thing.[10]

Kenney's point is well taken, even though he believes his perception to be evidence of a weakness in the novel. What it more probably indicates, however, is that Hammett may be doing something other than trying to write a traditional detective story. Hammett has not received the kind of critical attention he deserves partly because, like Kenney, too many commentators assume he must belong to a school of detective writers or to a particular tradition. Raymond Chandler put the problem most succinctly when he said that "Once in a long while a detective story writer is treated as a writer, but very seldom,"[11] and that what too often happens is that critics catalog stories rather than examining them thoroughly for their own merits.

Perhaps nothing so well illustrates Chandler's point than the fact that Edenbaum's, Malin's, and Grella's essays appear in a collection entitled *Tough Guy Writers of the Thirties*. Such cataloging is not necessarily suspect; in fact it is often extremely helpful, but it can indicate a narrowness of approach to a writer's work. Further, it is interesting that in each essay the emphasis is on showing Hammett to be a purveyor of the tough-guy *Weltanschauung*, but little or no attention is given to the question of what his intention may have been in constructing the plot as he does, or in how well he does it.

That critics see such apparently diverse qualities in Sam Spade may suggest that *The Maltese Falcon* is a flawed work or that Hammett's underlying conception has not been clearly discerned. I wish to offer the hypothesis that the novel has a very particular plot—a renunciation plot—and that the effect achieved is one of admiration for Spade. Hammett subjects his protagonist to severe moral temptations, and shows that he contains the potential for falling to the numerous lures presented in the novel if he so chooses. Brigid is, of course, his greatest temptation, and the power of the plot derives partly from Spade's vulnerability to her. His renunciation of her proposal at the end is shown to be extremely difficult for him, and it is because Hammett shows it to be so that we can rightly measure Spade's moral strength and courage in saying no.

Robert Edenbaum described detective work in *The Maltese Falcon* as "a metaphor for existence,"[12] but he is content to mean by it that the detective is tough enough to make his own terms of existence. He is right, as far as he goes, but Hammett's point in the novel is that Spade's detective work discovers not only a murderess but at the same time a basic truth concerning human relationships. The triumph of Hammett's plot is that the developing love relationship between Spade and Brigid is coherently tied to the investigation of his partner's murder and to the search for the falcon. Because Brigid O'Shaughnessy stands at the center of all three concerns, Spade's reaction to her at the end reflects very clearly what he has come to discover concerning the nature of external reality, and his relationship to it. The arrival of Spade at such knowledge is Hammett's central interest, and he uses detection as the means. It is in this fuller sense that detective work becomes a metaphor for existence.

[97]

Failure to perceive such coherence leads William Kenney to argue that *The Maltese Falcon* is a flawed work:

> The emotional climax of the novel is surely the scene in which Spade tells Brigid of his intention to turn her over to the police. Yet this scene grows out of what has been only a minor element in the plot, the murder of Miles Archer. The novel's main action, the quest for the falcon, reaches its climax with the discovery that

the bird is not genuine. There is then a structural division in the final episode of the novel, giving the scene
between Spade and Brigid, excellent as it is in itself,
almost the air of an afterthought.[13]

Kenney fails to perceive the cause and effect relationship
between the three stands of the plot, though he does see that
much of the action is "constructed as a series of ironic reversals"[14] and that this structural pattern suggests the "constant
need for reappraisal in human experience."[15]

It is surprising that Kenney should fail to see the unity of
The Maltese Falcon because he comes so very close to articu-
lating it. He admits that Spade throws Brigid over at the end
because he becomes aware their relationship has been based
entirely on deception and that therefore whatever good may
have been with them has been poisoned;[16] but he will later say
that the most serious flaw in the novel is

> the gap between the seriousness with which Spade's
> character is presented and the artificiality of the action
> in which he is involved. The potential human mean-
> ing of Spade's attempt to formulate and follow a viable
> code in an amoral environment is not fully realized
> because the environment in which beautiful interna-
> tional thieves exercise their cunning stratagems is too
> obviously of the stuff of romantic daydreams to reflect
> adequately the realities of human experience.[17]

One of the problems with such a reading is its narrow conception of Spade's "environment," a narrowness that originates
from the mistaken notion that the murder of Miles Archer is
only "a minor element in the plot" and that the main action is
the quest for the falcon.[18]

The generating question of the novel is: Who killed Miles Archer? Hammett employs his usual technique of exposition, showing that this narrowly conceived question has its answer in an extremely complex and ambiguous labyrinth of intentions and motives. As in *Red Harvest* and *The Dain Curse*, the initial crime in *The Maltese Falcon* proves to be only the beginning of a much more complicated case. In the Hammett world, crime proliferates outward, permeating various levels of society and threatening to engulf the detective.[19] The battle is not simply conceived as the good detective against the evil forces, as in television's *The Shield* or *Law & Order*. In Hammett's novels crime becomes more a gauntlet for testing the detective's inner strength and character. We found in *Red Harvest* that crime twisted the Op's perspective of himself and his world, and in *The Dain Curse* that crime twisted everyone but the Op (although we must say that Hammett kept his detective free of personal temptation and thus failed to thoroughly test his operative). But in *The Maltese Falcon* Hammett returns to his action-centered detective and shows through Spade's actions and reactions that ethical action is possible in a world of treachery and deceit, despite personal involvement.

The novel opens with a red herring. A "Miss Wonderly" appears in Spade's office and wishes to employ him on a missing person case. Supposedly Miss Wonderly's sister, Corinne, has run away with a bad-natured fellow called Floyd Thursby. Sam and Miles Archer take Wonderly's case, and that night Miles is murdered in an alley. Spade's initial question is: who killed his partner? This is the first strand of Hammett's triparte plot.

In her second scene in the novel, Miss Wonderly claims that her name is Brigid O'Shaughnessy. She admits her first story was a lie, and pleads for Sam's protection against evil forces that she says she cannot, for the present, identify for him. He will have to trust her. Although Sam perceives she is a good actress, he agrees nevertheless to become her protector—for an additional fee.[20] His decision to stand as her protector initiates the second strand of the novel's plot: the relationship between Sam and Brigid.

The appearance of the perfumed dandy Joel Cairo introduces the third plot strand: the quest for the Maltese falcon. Cairo urges Spade to accept five thousand dollars to get the bird back. Like the Continental Op before him, Spade makes his code of ethics clear from the outset: "You're not hiring me to do any murders or burglaries for you, but simply to get it back if possible in an honest and lawful way."[21] At this point Cairo asks that his gun be returned (Spade having wrestled it from him), and Spade, suspecting no betrayal, returns it, only to have the gun turned on him again.

In a very subtle way, Hammett has introduced within the first five chapters three plot strands, and has integrated them. Sam's trust in Cairo's good intentions suffers betrayal, and this reversal of expectation marks not only what will be seen to be a dominant theme in the novel, but reflects ironically on the preceding scene with Brigid. In her longest speech in that scene, she urges him to trust her:

[100]

> "Then can't you *trust* me a little?. . .I know I've no right to ask you to *trust* me if I won't *trust* you. I do *trust* you, but I can't tell you. . . . I'm afraid of *trusting* you. I don't mean that. I do *trust* you, but—I *trusted* Floyd. . ."[22]

Spade is not convinced. As he says to Effie Perine, his secretary: "She's got too many names,"[23] but though he cannot believe in her words, by agreeing to protect her and to put himself on the line for her, he indicates he is willing to trust in her basic goodness.

Robert Edenbaum would violently disagree. He argues that

> Spade baits Effie again and again by asking what
> her "woman's intuition" tells her about Brigid
> O'Shaughnessy; Effie is "for her;" "that girl is all
> right."[24]

But if we look at one of these baiting scenes carefully, we note
that Sam's responses are not as simple as Edenbaum suggests:

> "Does your woman's intuition still tell you that she's a
> madonna or something?"
>   She looked sharply up at him. "I still believe that
> no matter what kind of trouble she's gotten into she's all
> right, if that's what you mean."
>   "That what I mean."[25]

At the end of this scene, Sam asks Effie to put Brigid up for a
few days at her apartment because she is in some danger.

Although there is a bantering tone in this scene because of
Spade's exaggeration of Effie's view of Brigid as a "madonna,"
his concern seems real. He, too, thinks "she's all right," and
his intention to keep her with Effie certainly indicates that he
does not see her as a dangerous killer. Furthermore, and most
damaging to Edenbaum's argument, it would be pointless if, at
this juncture in the novel, Sam already knows Brigid is a murderess. We would be forced to regard him as a fool were this so;
it would mean that he allows himself to fall in love with her (or
very close to it) and then, at the end, to stand up and repudiate
her for her falseness. That would be stupid and unconvincing.
He knows, for example, that Iva Archer is a bitch and, though
he has been willing to sleep with her in the past, it is clear
he has no feeling for her.[26] But there is an emphasis on Sam's

[101]

growing feeling for Brigid, an emphasis hardly consistent with his clear-sightedness which Edenbaum posits by arguing that he knows almost from the beginning that she is guilty.

The entire emphasis in the first half of the novel is, in fact, on Spade's obvious desire to want to believe in Brigid despite all the evidence he gathers to the contrary. He knows she isn't what she pretends to be, but her lying is not what bothers him as much as her refusal to give him some indication that below her words lie some kind of substance or truth:

> Spade laughed. His laughter was brief and somewhat bitter. "That is good," he said, "coming from you. What have you given me besides money? Have you given me any of your confidence? any of the truth? any help in helping you? Haven't you tried to buy my loyalty with money and nothing else?"[27]

Spade's bitterness is the bitterness of a man who hopes to find something other than he would normally (and cynically) expect and keeps finding himself disappointed. He wants a sign, an indication that his confidence will not be violated. Amoral men do not talk in such a manner; they do not posit values of moral substance. Spade does. Brigid fails to understand what he is really asking for; she responds by asking, "Can I buy you with my body?"[28]—a response that makes him contemptuous and angry:

> "I don't give a damn about your honesty," he told her, trying to make himself speak calmly. "I don't care what kind of tricks you're up to, what your secrets are, but I've got to have something to show that you know what you're doing." . . . "I'm willing to help you. I've done what I could so far. If necessary I'll go ahead blind-folded, but I can't do it without more confidence in you

than I've got now. You've got to convince me that you know what it's all about, that you're not simply fiddling around by guess and by God, hoping it'll come out all right somehow in the end."[29]

He demands to know what is going on; if he is to back her, he needs to know she is not playing games. He needs a reason to have confidence in her if he is to act for her. As he puts it, "You don't have to trust me, anyhow, as long as you can persuade me to trust you."[30]

The three plot strands become more clearly interwoven when Brigid reveals to Sam that she too is trying to recover the Maltese falcon. What she tells Sam in the chapter entitled "Brigid" are lies, as he well sees, but some truth is there: Brigid is part of the search for the falcon. She and Joel Cairo are, therefore, connected, though their precise relationship remains cloudy. Miles Archer's death is still unaccounted for, but we now see that it must be tied in with the falcon affair. The three stands are also held together through the linking of Thursby and Brigid. Thursby is a central figure in Brigid's first story and is therefore seemingly connected with the murder of Miles Archer. In her second story to Spade, Thursby is her reputed traveling companion from the Orient whom she suspects of killing Miles. This lie, as it later turns out, is her gambit for gaining Spade's sympathy and protection, and thus an important element in plot-strand two. Since Thursby is mentioned by Cairo as a competitor for the falcon, it is more than likely that Brigid has an interest in it too. The reader is fairly certain, as is Spade, by the end of Chapter V that the falcon quest and Brigid's troubles are related.

In short, the quest for the falcon slowly emerges as the center for all the unanswered questions in the novel: Who killed Miles? What is Brigid really mixed up in? What is the relationship between Cairo and Casper Gutman? And what does Brigid want with Sam Spade? The falcon comes to stand for the labyrinthian and complex motivation in which the initial question of the novel—who killed Miles?—finds its answer.

The Maltese falcon is described and its pedigree given by the smooth talking, bibulous fat villain, Casper Gutman, in Chapter XIII, "The Emperor's Gift." One of the interesting things about its supposed history is that it has served as a symbol for so many diverse qualities: loyalty, responsibility, greed, love, nobility, disguise, and murder. It began as a symbol of the unswerving loyalty of the Order of the Hospital of St. John of Jerusalem on Malta to the Spanish Emperor Charles V. Stolen by buccaneers, the falcon appeared one hundred years later in the possession of Sir Francis Verney of England. It next appeared in 1713 in the possession of King Victor Amadeus II, who gave it to his wife as a token of his love. For two hundred years it surfaced intermittently, appearing in Paris during the Carlist revolution. At this time it was disguised, its gold and jewels painted over to look like any common artifact. As Gutman tells it, its real value wasn't discovered until 1911 by a Greek antique dealer. He was murdered, and the falcon was stolen, not seen again until Gutman chased it down seventeen years later in Constantinople, this time in the possession of a Russian general. Gutman sent agents after it, but he has not heard of it since, and he now wants Spade to locate it.

Critics have had a good deal to say about the nature and function of this falcon. Irving Malin suggests that it represents the metaphysical:

> The more we learn about it, the more "metaphysical" it becomes. This is the secret—the falcon changes...it is *a changing symbol of change itself.* It can never really be grasped; it vanishes triumphantly.[31]

William Nolan quotes Ross Macdonald as having said about it:

> The black bird is hollow, worthless. The reality behind
> appearance is a treacherous vacuum...the bird's lack
> of value implies Hammett's final comment on the
> inadequacy and superficiality of Spade's life and ours. If
> only his bitterly inarticulate struggle for self-realization
> were itself more fully realized...Sam Spade could
> have become a great indigenous tragic figure...I think
> *The Maltese Falcon*...is tragedy of a new kind, dead-
> pan tragedy.[32]

Though both are interesting comments, I think neither perceives the full subtlety of Hammett's symbol. By the end of the
novel, we see that the falcon's history finds substantiality in the
action even if not in real historical terms. The falcon's qualities
are reflected in every character. Among other things, the falcon
is a bird of prey, and as such it symbolizes not only the rapacious natures of Gutman, Cairo, Wilmer Cook, and Brigid, but
also the violence and brutality of all those who (if the history
can be believed) connived to possess it. The bird's historical
connection with love and romance is repeated in Sam's love for
Brigid and Brigid's use of the romantic lure to entrap Sam, and
its association with nobility is repeated in Spade's noble adherence to his code and in Gutman's phony aristocratic manners.
The falcon's elusiveness, moreover, connects with the dominant
problem of the novel: knowing reality.

    Seen this way, the falcon becomes first and foremost a
symbol of the human condition—its best and worst potentiali-
ties. Most importantly, it becomes symbolic of the problematic
nature of reality. It is assumed to be an object of great value, and
Hammett's characters design their plans, attitudes, and actions
around this assumption. But it turns out to be a fake, a phony,

worth only its weight in lead. Hammett even leaves the reality of the real falcon in doubt. The long and involved history and pedigree may be pure romance—a fantasy. The irony is that Brigid, Gutman, and the rest have lied, cheated, and murdered in their pursuit of this object, and all for nothing. This is poetic justice in itself. Hammett implies that one's perception of a thing becomes its reality for him, but the nature of perception and its relationship to action is complicated, in this case, because the object that precipitates the action in the novel is never actually seen. *The Maltese Falcon* is largely about the problem of detecting reality and the problem of acting according to one's own apprehension of the way things are, and Hammett's treatment of the falcon throughout suggests the danger—and even foolishness—of trusting external images.

If the falcon symbolized the ways of seeing and acting of most of the characters in *The Maltese Falcon*, Sam Spade's parabolic story of Flitcraft in Chapter VII is about the way someone else saw reality and who, because of a fortuitous event, came to see that his view of the way things worked in the world had little or no basis in fact. His new perception most clearly represents Sam Spade's own view of reality. The Flitcraft story and the Maltese falcon are not opposing emblems; their meanings reinforce one another, but the Flitcraft tale reflects a vision of reality that is more focused because it is simplified and grounded in the practical work-a-day world.

Spade tells Brigid the story right after she has insisted that he must trust her. Though he has tried to force her to admit some truth, she has resisted his probings. The story is told in Spade's "matter-of-fact voice," and concerns a case he worked on years before. Flitcraft, a man with a twenty-five thousand a year job, a wife and child, and a home in the suburbs, on his way to work narrowly escapes being hit by a beam falling from eight stories up. This chance escape dramatically alters his view of life as sane and orderly, and demonstrates to him that in ordering his affairs he had gotten out of step with life. [33] Flitcraft now realizes that man lives only while blind chance spares him. As a result, he leaves his family and disappears, only to surface years later again remarried and settled in suburbia. Spade explains to Brigid:

> "He wasn't sorry for what he had done. It seemed reasonable enough to him. I don't think he even knew he had settled back naturally into the same groove he had jumped out of in Tacoma. But that's the part of it I always liked. He adjusted himself to beams falling, and then no more of them fell, and he adjusted himself to them not falling."[34]

William Kenney takes the anecdote to be an example of the doctrine that "the man who thinks he can plan his life and control his destiny is a fool." He also argues that the "final irony of Flitcraft's story is that his insight and his decision to act on his insight prove as meaningless as anything else in a universe of chance."[35] Irving Malin sees a connection between the Flitcraft story and the falcon because they both reflect the impermanency of identities in the novel.[36] Robert Edenbaum goes even further by suggesting that the anecdote represents the "naturalistic conception of the randomness of the universe [that] is Spade's vision throughout." According to him, Spade lives "by Flitcraft's vision of meaninglessness and the hard knowingness that follows from that vision."[37]

Kenney's perception that Flitcraft's discovery about the true nature of life is seeing that man cannot presume to know or control his own reality is interesting and quite accurate. Certainly one thing the anecdote tells us is that life is unpredictable and uncertain. It is similar to Hamlet's perception after the sea voyage and the graveyard scene:

"We defy augury. There's special providence in the fall of a sparrow. If it be now, 'tis not to come. If it be not to come, it will be now. If it be not now, yet it will come. The readiness is all. Since no man knows aught of what he leaves, what is't to betimes? Let be."[38]

But to then argue that the meaninglessness of life is all one can be sure of is to miss the point all together. Edenbaum makes a similar error by assuming that Spade follows such a vision. More likely, the story suggests that the external world lacks certainty, and therefore one must not count on the stability of anything outside one's self. Flitcraft discovers that his previous life has been a lie because he has acted on false assumptions concerning the nature of the world. Therefore he determines he must act in such a way as to free himself from reliance on such false security. Critic John Paterson remarks that the Flitcraft story approximates

the central experience of the age, the experience of a war epoch, of an age of transition in which men are less confident of their values and their motives, less pleased with the society they have constructed.[39]

[108] Flitcraft's new vision is not one of meaninglessness, but of meaning, and it reflects not only Spade's sense that order is no longer a viable quality of the external world but Hammett's sense as well.

Hammett seems to imply that one's freedom lies in what one does, and what one does is necessitated by how one sees the world. The meaning of the Flitcraft parable is that if one can see clearly enough to understand that external reality is unstable and unpredictable, then one must be ready to react to its ironies. As Hamlet put it after coming to a similar recognition, "the readiness is all." Hamlet's madness was partly the madness of acting as if the world were predictable enough to attempt to shape destinies and control events; Flitcraft's life up to the moment the beam fell reflects a similar madness. But with the fall of the beam he reacts according to his new perception. Hammett's point here is that it is not enough to simply recognize truth; one must act upon it, and so he has Flitcraft leave everything that he had created while living under the illusion. When beams no longer fall, he readjusts his vision and creates a family life very similar to the one he left.

Flitcraft's return to a life exactly parallel to the one he left is the most problematic element of the story. How has he changed? It may be that Hammett wishes to suggest that his "second" life is truer than his first because in the first instance beams fell and he was not prepared but here in the second he has experienced his world as one in which beams do not fall and therefore he can rely on a certain pattern of order. But equally, I think, Hammett intends us to see the parable as an illustration of the difference between Flitcraft's life and Sam Spade's. For a moment only, Flitcraft experienced the world of the detective, a world in which beams are forever likely to fall. Flitcraft has the luxury of not having to live according to his new knowledge that the world is (or can be) terrifyingly unpredictable; his world does not often enough reveal itself as that. But Spade's does, and one senses in his attraction to Flitcraft's unknowing return to his old ways perhaps a sense of envy, the envy of an outsider regarding a being in a different world.

At any rate, to some extent the Flitcraft parable, like the Maltese falcon, stands for the absurdity of assuming that the external world in necessarily stable. Both illustrate the problematic nature of reality. The parable points more to the inescapable loneliness and uncertainty of Spade's life, a life that most of us share only in brief moments, whereas the Maltese falcon symbolizes the impermanency of all external objects and patterns.

[109]

Significantly, it is the object that everyone but Spade uses to determine his actions. The irony is that Gutman, Brigid, Cairo, and Wilmer are slaves to their conceptions of it, thus making them just as unaware and unprepared as Flitcraft before his beam fell. In a very real sense, they have no reality because their selves are defined wholly in terms of their reliance on, and perception of, the shimmering falcon.

In fact, Hammett's very method of characterizing the four conspirators indicates their lack of inner reality. William Kenney argues that they

> do not share Spade's complexity, but are drawn with a clarity based on intelligent simplification. To achieve this clarity, Hammett resorts successfully to the device of providing each character with a distinct and individual style of speech.[40]

We know them by the way they speak. Their words suggest what they wish to appear to be: Gutman's jovial and aristocratic pose; Brigid's helpless and sensuous one; Wilmer's tough rhetoric; and Cairo's oily and pretentious veneer. But there is no clarity here. In each case their words belie their real natures. Words fly up but deeds go along the ground, and what the conspirators say has little or no relationship to what they are. Walter Blair describes this as Hammett's "association of deceptive images and descriptive details with the characters," which gives them outward aspects incongruous with their actual natures.[41] Gutman turns out to be a cruel and ruthless man in his actions; despite his fatherly rhetoric concerning Wilmer he is all too willing to turn him over to the police if it means his greed for the falcon can be satisfied. Wilmer's tough rhetoric belies his childish nature. Although he kills two people in the novel—Thursby and Captain Jacobi—he is impotent before

Spade and Gutman in the final scenes. His tough pose disintegrates, and the last we see of him he is running away. Beneath Cairo's perfumed appearance lies a vicious and degenerate nature. Beneath Brigid's helpless girl-in-need role lies a scheming, tough, murderous mind.

The language and appearance of the four villains, then, are as ambiguous and unreliable as the Maltese falcon itself. There are those critics who scoff at *The Maltese Falcon* because, in the words of one, "Judged even by the lenient standards of mystery fiction its characters are parodies of Hammett's blend of romantic adventurousness and stoic coolness."[42] But I would rather stress that in presenting a "romantic" and exotic cast of characters, Hammett has so treated them that we see them critically, not as real romantic figures but as people beguiled by their own romantic notions of how the universe works. Because they are as capable of deceiving themselves as they are in deceiving others, they prove vulnerable to Sam Spade.

Hammett's handling of Spade's physical characteristics deserves attention because there is subtlety to it that is lacking in his rendering of the others. Sam, too, seems to have been given his "handle": he is "a blond Satan," has tigerish yellow eyes, and grins "wolfishly." Yet at the same time he is described as a large, powerful man whose style exudes confidence and control. Hammett puts it this way:

> Spade's thick fingers made a cigarette with deliberate care, sifting a measured quantity of tan flakes down into curved paper, spreading the flakes so that they lay equal at the ends with a slight depression in the middle, thumbs rolling the paper's inner edge down and up under the outer edge as forefingers pressed it over, thumbs and fingers sliding to the paper cylinder's ends to hold it even while tongue licked the flap, left

forefinger and thumb pinching their end, right forefinger and thumb twisting their end and lifting the other to Spade's mouth.[43]

This is Spade's initial reaction to the news that Miles Archer has been killed. I quote at some length because Hammett's third person narration of Spade's actions rolling a cigarette etch clearly in the reader's mind his essential character. The labels—blond Satan, tigerish eyes, and the wolfish grin—represent what his appearance is to others. As such it resembles the tough, survival-of-the fittest role that Wilmer imitates, and that Brigid, Gutman, and Cairo find so appealing in Spade. He indeed appears to be a man who might be a suitable protector, or partner in a corrupt enterprise. He appears to be tough, ruthless, corruptible—characteristics which encourage the villains to think he can be used profitably.

But the irony is that the conspirators see Spade no more clearly than they see themselves or the Maltese falcon. We see Spade's complexity. Hammett's description of Spade making and lighting a cigarette illustrates Spade's controlled and deliberate character; he is a man rooted in the real world of detail and cold fact. We know him by what he does; his private actions define who and what he is. In a chaotic world, a man must make his own stability. The ceremonial quality of Spade's actions reflect his method of creating his own personal order within instability. Donald Phelps has said that Hammett's Op and his other heroes become the center of their own universe, its fulcrum, and its magnetic pole.[44] Spade's reaction to Miles' death is shown through his actions, not his feelings. He never liked Miles, and we sense this in his reaction. It seems action is equated with truth in Spade. With the other characters, neither their actions nor their words are reliable clues to their natures.

Actions, then, falsify less than words. Although the villains' actions are misleading, Hammett shows us that what they *do* in the novel is false, a role adopted to conform to their chosen verbal masks. Most of their real actions—their violent murders and degenerate practices—happen either before the novel opens or take place off-stage and we don't see them in private. It is part of Spade's job to detect their real natures by uncovering the truth of what they have *done*. The verbal screens and misleading actions of the conspirators have him perplexed throughout most of the novel. As he says to Brigid:. . . "I've got to keep in some sort of touch with all the loose ends of this dizzy affair if I'm ever going to make heads or tails of it."[45]

Hammett arranges his plot in what initially seems to be a very misleading fashion. A series of intricately false complications lead and mislead Spade and the reader until the discovery scene, Chapter XX. Besides adding the proper ingredients of mystification and suspense necessary for any good mystery story, these complications illustrate the difficulty of finding truth in a false world, and indicate the qualities requisite for survival in such a world.

I count nine major deceptions. The first four have already been mentioned.

1. Brigid as "Miss Wonderly" is the first.
2. Her accusation against Thursby as Miles' killer is the second.
3. The third is the police view that Spade had a hand in Miles' death, a view momentarily strengthened when we learn he has been seeing Iva Archer secretly, that Iva called the police, and that her brother believes him to be guilty.
4. The fourth appears in Chapter IX, where Brigid tells Spade a series of lies connecting Thursby and herself to

the Maltese falcon. We are led to believe that she is a helpless victim of his greed.

5. Fifth, in Chapter XII we are led to believe that foul play may account for Brigid's mysterious disappearance, a red herring which accounts for Spade's belief that her phone call for help in Chapter XVI is legitimate—the seventh false lead.

6. The sixth again involves the police: they believe that a gambler's revenge drama is the cause of all the trouble (Chapter XV).

7. The false phone call for help is mentioned above.

8. The eighth is the Rhea Gutman scene which leads Spade on another wild goose chase.

9. The ninth is the supposedly missing one thousand dollar bill in Chapter XIX. What appears to be Brigid's theft turns out to be a controlled test given to Spade by Gutman. Spade doesn't fall for it and when the trick is discovered, our growing suspicion of Brigid is somewhat dissipated. She again appears clean.

We must add a tenth. The discovery that the Maltese falcon is a phony shows it to be very much a part of the red herring world of the novel. The climatic irony is that the actions of the conspirators prove to be not only a masquerade for Spade's benefit, but worthless and empty even in their own world. Because they have based all their actions on a false supposition concerning the falcon, they do no escape the fall of their beam.

These ten incidents involve all three plot strands—Miles' death, Brigid and Spade, and the quest for the Maltese falcon—and connect the three environments of the novel: the world of the police, the world of the conspirators, and the world of Sam Spade. William Kenney's complaint that the action in the novel is "artificial' stems from his narrow conception of the plot and a failure to see that the unreal quality of the events in the novel is precisely Hammett's point.[46] The plot is larger and more inclusive than the schemes of the villains. The police are even more unclear than Spade about where the truth lies, and Spade himself is led in circles during his investigation. The villains, too, are finally shown to have completely mistaken falsehood as truth. Everyone in the novel, from District Attorney Bryan to Effie Perine—who never accepts the full truth about Brigid—to Brigid herself in the final scenes, is mistaken in their conceptions of the truth. Hammett has rendered a fictional landscape that illustrates, at every turn, how difficult it is to find the path to truth—any truth—and how ironic it is when man, believing himself to be in possession of the truth, creates artificial patterns which have no basis in reality.

But Spade's job is by definition to find truth. In order for him to act in the real world, he must appear to be part of it. Like the conspirators, Sam plays a variety of roles, and becomes an expert at the art of illusion and role-playing. But there is a difference. Every role he plays has a clear correlation with his real nature. Spade's fictions, like his story of Flitcraft, are always rooted in the hard, cold world of fact; and this is one reason he is able to retain control over his antagonists. For example, in the chapter "Horse Feathers," Spade improvises brilliantly to keep himself, Brigid, and Cairo from going to jail. He not only verbally out-maneuvers the police but gains the upper hand because he is able to control his feelings under pressure. Lieutenant Dundy, in his shame at being stymied by Spade's rendition of the happenings in the room, loses his temper and slugs Spade. As Spade tells Brigid: "It was that in losing his head and slugging me he overplayed his hand."[47] Like the villains, Dundy is inflexible, ruled by his passions as much as they are by their greed, and therefore he is vulnerable to someone who is more flexible and aware of the exigencies of the situation.

[115]

Time and time again Spade demonstrates such control. It is not that he lacks feelings, as some have argued.[48] I see no reason to doubt his rage following the scene with Dundy:

> Red rage came suddenly into his face and he began to talk in a harsh guttural voice. Holding his maddened face in his hands, glaring at the floor, he cursed Dundy for five minutes without a break, cursed him obscenely, blasphemously, repetitiously, in a harsh guttural voice.[49]

As he says to Brigid: ". . . I do hate being hit without hitting back," but it is "a cheap enough price to pay for winning."[50] Winning is the point, and Spade possesses the ability of Ben Jonson's rogues: to keep distance and maintain perspective.

Spade is an imaginative role player. He creates out of impulses and intuition. When Gutman appears to hire him to recover the falcon, Spade forces Gutman to play his game:

> "Maybe you could have got along without me if you'd kept clear of me. You can't now. Not in San Francisco. You'll come in or you'll get out—and you'll do it today."[51]

His new role is to appear tough but vulnerable. In contrast to Gutman's bland and controlled veneer, Spade plays almost a Dundy role—he loses his temper—and Gutman falls for it. In a later scene, confident he can outwit Spade, Gutman drugs him and tries to work alone, thus creating enough ripples of action—the meeting with Brigid and Jacobi on the ship and the shooting of Jacobi, as well as the Rhea Gutman incident—for Spade to trace.

Ironically, it is Casper Gutman's precipitous action that eventually gives Spade his most potent weapon: the black bird.

Dying, Jacobi leaves it with Spade, and in Chapters XVIII and XIX Spade plays his most brilliant roles. Edenbaum argues that his real power lies in his ability to "rob a Gutman of his ultimate weapon, the threat of death."[52] He argues further that

> When Gutman threatens Spade, the detective can argue that the fat man needs him alive; Gutman returns that there are other ways to get information; Spade, in his turn, insists that there is no terror without the threat of death, that he can play Gutman so that the fat man will not kill him, but that if need be he can *force* Gutman to kill him. Who but the tough guy can *make* the beam fall? In that lies the tough guy's power to set his own terms in life and death, a power that is the basis for his popularity in detective and other fiction.[53]

Nicely put, if all you want to do is further a thesis arguing that Spade is an archetypal tough guy, but in its neat formulation it obscures more than it clarifies. Hammett's point in these scenes is surely not that Spade is merely unafraid of death; rather, the emphasis is on Spade's psychological manipulation of Gutman, Cairo, and Wilmer. He knows he can force them to his will because he knows the extent of their greed. For example, when Wilmer wants to "fog" him, Spade only smiles and says:

[117]

> "Young Wild West." His voice matched his smile. "Maybe you ought to tell him that shooting me before you get your hands on the falcon would be bad for business."[54]

He knows they can't "afford" to kill him. He plays them off against one another in a manner very reminiscent of the Op in *Red Harvest*. Spade's power is not so much his contempt of death as it is his knowledge of his enemies. Knowing that greed is the most powerful passion in Gutman, he knows he is safe because Gutman is completely predictable. His careless attitude towards death is more rhetorical than real:

> "Like hell I must." Spade flung his words out with a brutal sort of carelessness that gave them more weight than they could have got from dramatic emphasis or from loudness.[55]

Spade's real power is knowing the way things are.

The main business of Chapters XVIII and XIX is Spade's discovery of the central unanswered questions of the novel: Who killed Miles? Who killed Thursby, who killed Jacobi, and what is Brigid's real connection with the falcon? Spade pretends to be one of the villains, willing to accept payment for the bird and to trick the police. Here again critics have failed to see through Spade's role:

> Paradoxically, in *The Maltese Falcon* the good guy is a "blonde satan" and the villain is as innocent as she pretends to be. For that matter Gutman, Cairo, even Wilmer, are appalled by Spade, and in their inability to cope with him are as innocent as Brigid.[56]

Spade's role-playing has a point, however. His pretense for the need of a "fall guy" is his method of probing for the truth of who shot who and why. Were Spade as corrupt as some critics would have it,[57] why would he bother with all this? Why wouldn't he simply take Gutman's money and turn over the bird? Surely his intention in these scenes is to discover some answers. By suggesting Wilmer for fall guy, Spade can force Gutman to construct plausible reasons why the police might

be convinced and accept him as the murderer of Miles and
Thursby. Spade says,

> "If, as is likely enough, he used the same gun on both,
> the bullets will match up. Everybody will be satisfied."
> "Yes, but—" Gutman began, and stopped to look
> at the boy.[58]

Gutman resists the suggestion, so Spade suggests Cairo. But
again Gutman resists. So far Spade hasn't gained much information, but it is clear from his method of phrasing his suggestions
in the hypothetical if-then form that he is experimenting with
theories in order to get information.

To speed the process of detection, Spade needles the
hot-tempered Wilmer until he drives him to pull a gun. At
this point, faced with a loss of profit, Gutman reacts, and
turns against Wilmer. Spade has successfully driven a wedge
between the antagonistic forces and is in full control. With
Wilmer's overreaction, Spade has made Gutman play his
hand, and has his fall guy. Now he can force details to the
surface:

> "Let's get the details fixed. Why did he shoot Thursby?
> And why and where and how did he shoot Jacobi?"[59]

Again Gutman resists, trying to cover up, and Spade says:

> "A fall-guy is what I asked for, and he's not a fall-guy
> unless he's a cinch to take the fall. Well, to cinch that
> I've got to know what's what."[60]

Pushed, Gutman now admits both men were shot with Wilmer's
gun, but Spade demands more information:

[119]

"Maybe," Spade agreed, "but the thing's more complicated than that and I've got to know what happened so I
can be sure the parts that won't fit in are covered up."[61]

What stands out here is not Spade's actual corruptness, only his
pretense, an adopted role fashioned to probe for the truth.

The information Spade gets is necessary for his perception
in the final chapters that Brigid is the one he has been hunting
all along. Spade forces Gutman to reveal that she and Jacobi
had once before slipped away with the falcon, that his death
was her fault, that Wilmer had in fact shot Thursby and Jacobi,
and that Brigid cannot be trusted. The only part that doesn't fit
in, the only unanswered question, is: Who killed Miles Archer?
From what he has learned in the previous chapter, Spade can
eliminate everyone but Brigid, and now he knows all answers.[62]
Before this point, he cannot know for sure.

The scene in which Spade discovers that the falcon is a
phony is also the scene in which he perceives the extent of
Brigid's falseness. The end of the quest for the falcon reveals
the impossibility of the Spade-Brigid relationship, and therefore
I do not see the "structural division" that Kenney sees.[63] Hammett has woven his plot in such a manner that the question
of who killed Miles is shown to be integrally tied in with the
quest for the falcon—the former is the impetus for searching for
the latter—and the discovery of the truth of the falcon's value
discovers the murderer of Miles. The last discovery is Spade's
alone, and his reaction to it defines the measure of a man in
Hammett's universe.

Before analyzing Spade's rejection of Brigid in the final
chapter, a clearer understanding of their relationship prior to
the discovery is necessary. Few critics are willing to assert that
Sam is in love with Brigid.[64] Most hedge on the issue, but I suggest that Hammett means us to take their relationship seriously.

Not to do so makes the final scene not only void of emotional impact, but redundant as well.

Spade's concern for Brigid in the early sections of the novel has already been mentioned: he protects her from the police even though he has no need to; he tries desperately to make her level with him so he can more effectively help her; and he tries to send her to live with Effie to shield her from danger. We don't have to deny his skepticism about her to say that he seems, underneath it all, to concur with Effie that "she's all right."

Through the middle sections of the novel, this same concern is evident, and their intimacy increases. He protects her from District Attorney Bryan.[65] Between Chapters IX and X he sleeps with her. Hammett never lets us inside his mind, however, and this certainly accounts for the uncertainty of the critics. Spade's actions the morning after he sleeps with Brigid anticipate the final scene. Despite the love-making, he is capable of getting up early to search her rooms blocks away and then return with breakfast and a kiss. As he later sees, he finds an important clue—her week-old receipt for a month's apartment rent—but at this point in the novel Hammett does not point out that it is evidence of her guilt.[66]

Though Spade is methodical in his desire to search out the truth concerning Brigid, he is not cold. She has hired him, but not given him much to go on except lies. Searching her rooms could as well indicate a desire to find her innocent of all wrongdoings as well as guilty, but we can't be sure. Hammett won't tell us, so we can only judge by his actions. He sleeps with her, yes, but he also slept with Iva Archer; but he spends time with Brigid, none with Iva. He stops seeing Iva when he begins seeing Brigid.

Yet professionalism seems to dominate Spade's actions. In one scene he makes her strip in order to determine whether she stole the thousand-dollar bill. He may know Gutman is testing him, in which case he must go through with it or fail; or he may not know, just as easily; we cannot be sure. What we can be sure of is that his need to "know" is most important to him: ". . . I've got to know."[67] Truth is more important than maidenly modesty; in the final scene we see it is more important than love. Hammett shows in that final scene that truth to one's profession, truth to the way things are, and truth to one's self all become one. Hammett's moral vision in *The Maltese Falcon* can only be understood in these terms.

Raymond Chandler said that Hammett "did over and over again what only the best writers can ever do at all. He wrote scenes that seemed never to have been written before."[68]

Such a scene is Spade's final confrontation with Brigid in Chapter XX. It is the most moving section of the novel. At this point Spade has all the pieces of the puzzle assembled; he knows the truth, and though he must battle his emotions fiercely to do it, he adheres to his truth. Hammett's emphasis is not on his demonic quality, as Edenbaum would have it, but on his very real struggle with himself to resist his feeling for Brigid and to hold on to what he knows is true.

What he has discovered is simply this: Brigid had hired Miles in the hope that Thursby would try to kill Miles. If Thursby did try, the police would be after him, and she would be free to keep the falcon to herself. Or, if Thursby missed Miles and Miles killed Thursby, she would also be free. When Thursby didn't kill Miles, she does; but when Thursby is killed she knows she is in danger from Gutman's people and she runs to Spade for protection.

The most important aspect of the scene, however, is Hammett's subtle rendering of Spade's growing personal anguish during it. First Spade hits her with the facts, and then Hammett tells us:

Spade said *tenderly*: "You angel! Well, if you get a good break you'll be out of San Quentin in twenty years and you can come back to me then."

He was *pale*. He said *tenderly*: "I hope to Christ they don't hang you, precious, by that sweet neck." He slid his hands up to caress her throat.[69]

A few lines later, he says:

"I'm going to send you over. The chances are you'll get off with life., That means you'll be out again in twenty years. You're an angel. I'll wait for you." He cleared his throat. "If they hang you I'll always remember you."[70]

Though these lines may sound like clichés now, they were a first in the 1930s, and unless your own cynicism gets in the way, what comes through here is the strength of his feeling for her. The repeated word "tenderly" and the reference to his pale face suggests a great deal of feeling below his words. Hammett's diction is as it has been throughout—a behavioral clue. He focuses our attention on indirect signs of feeling:

[123]

Spade laughed. His yellow-white face was damp with sweat and though he held his smile he could not hold softness in his voice. He croaked: "Don't be silly. You're taking the fall."[71]

Spade's smile is his mask, but it is not totally intact. The clear emphasis in these lines is not his hardness but on his effort not to succumb to his feelings. He sweats with the effort.

A few lines later he admits as much as he ever will that he loves her—"I think I do"[72]—but he says he won't play the "sap"

CHAPTER FIVE ♠ THE MALTESE FALCON

for her. Seeing clearly that she came into his bed in order to stop him asking questions, he stresses the fact that she has never leveled with him:

> "I should trust you? You who arranged that nice little trick for—for my predecessor, Thursby? You who knocked off Miles, a man you had nothing against, in cold blood, just like swatting a fly, for the sake of double-crossing Thursby? You who double-crossed Gutman, Cairo, Thursby—one, two, three? You who've never played square with me for half an hour at a stretch since I've known you? I should trust you? No, no, darling. I wouldn't do it even if I could. Why should I?"[73]

He stresses her cold-bloodedness and her violation of trust, something he has been concerned about throughout the novel.

But despite his knowledge of her ruthless character, Spade finds it increasingly difficult to respond to her references to their love:

> Blood streaked Spade's eyeballs now and his long-held smile had become a frightful grimace. He cleared his throat huskily and said: "Making speeches is no damned good now." He put a hand on her shoulder. The hand shook and jerked. "I don't care who loves who . . . I can't help you now. And I wouldn't if I could."[74]

Practically every word reveals Spade's emotional effort. He does care who loves who, but he cares about truth more. I stress Hammett's gradual and increasingly poignant portrayal of Spade's emotional battle because it has either been ignored or overlooked by the majority of commentators. William Kenney's only remark is:

When Sam Spade tells Brigid he is sending her over,
we are informed of what Spade says, of the tone of his
voice, and of his facial expressions and gestures. We
may infer his feelings from these clues, but Hammett
says nothing directly about those feelings.[75]

For that matter, much the same could be said about Henry James'
characters. The power this scene lies in what is not said but inti-
mated, and we must attempt to elucidate the unsaid but implied
if we are to understand Hammett's intention in the novel. It is
only by assessing the depth of Spade's emotional strain that we
can rightly estimate the quality of his renunciation.

While "His wet yellow face was set hard and deeply lined,"[76]
Spade attempts for a final time to explain to her what he is and
why he must do what he intends. She was unable earlier to
understand the Flitcraft parable, so he becomes very specific
here. He gives seven reasons why he must turn her in, and the
full range of the Spade code is made clear in this enunciation.

- Reason one: "When a man's partner is killed he's
  supposed to do something about it;"
- Reason two: It's bad for the detective business to let
  "the killer get away;"
- "Third, I'm a detective and expecting me to run
  criminals down and then let them go free is like
  asking a dog to catch a rabbit and let it go. . . . it's not
  the natural thing;"[77]
- Reason four: If he lets her go he would be sent to the
  gallows himself;
- Reason five: He can't trust her;
- Reason six: Since he has "something on" her, she
  might shoot him some day; and,
- Reason seven: He can't stand the thought that she
  played him for a sucker.

Against all these reasons stands one: ". . . maybe you love me and maybe I love you."[78]

The seven reasons are interesting because they bridge moral and professional and personal concerns. Spade's code, his ethic, is to a large degree a work ethic. Reasons one, two and three are all professional, and he implies here as he has throughout the novel that a great part of his identity is inextricably a part of what he does for a living.[79] If he violates that, who or what is he? The tough-guy detective, like Nietzsche's Zarathustra, begins with his own existence as the reference point for all other reality. As Spade indicates, to go against the very purpose of his vocation is against natural law; it would make him analogous to Flitcraft before the fall of the beam. Seen this way, the professional reason becomes a personal one as well: to go counter to natural law is to deny the validity of one's perception of the way things are. Hammett consistently portrays Spade as one who sees more clearly than others. Brigid's appeal, for all its romantic dressing, is an appeal for self-denial. This Spade cannot and will not do. By affirming his existence as a detective, he affirms his own authenticity.

Reasons four through seven are all personal: they concern the art of survival. Reason seven—he can't stand to be played for a sucker—has to do with self-survival. The implication is that one must possess integrity of self to survive one's own self-appraisal. There is an almost quasi-existential emphasis here. Sartre has said that "Before you come alive, life is nothing: it's up to you to give it a meaning, and value is nothing else but the meaning that you choose."[80] Spade makes a *choice* in this final scene: he chooses to reaffirm his past existence. Maurice Friedman commenting on Ortega y Gasset argues that "vocation" is personal: "its meaning is always that of calling the person into authentic existence."[81] This is Hammett's point in having Spade define himself: "Your Sam's a detective."[82] Detective work is engagement with corrupt reality, a commitment to search out the truth, and Brigid's plea is that he disengage, ignore truth and become an inauthentic man. This he refuses to do.

Reason five—that Brigid has violated trust—posits a value and is therefore moral in its emphasis. The implication is that personal relationships must be based on trust if they are to be meaningful. The point Brigid defines for us by missing—she should have "got it"—is that love without truth is hollow, a sham. Realizing that she cannot fully understand what he is saying, he tells her to forget it all and to take what he means this way:

> "I won't because all of me wants to—wants to say to hell with the consequences and do it—and because—God damn you—you've counted on that with me the same as you counted on that with others."[83]

Robert Edenbaum insists on seeing these lines as evidence that the point of the novel is simply a confrontation between a woman of sentiment and a man without sentiment.[84]

But that is too simplified. First of all, these lines illustrate Spade's sentiment, not his lack of it. Secondly, they illustrate Spade's recognition that her actions toward him have been the same as toward other men, thus invalidating her argument that their relationship is something special. Thirdly, and most importantly, Spade's diction ("If that doesn't mean anything to you forget it and we'll make it this") certainly implies that he is over-simplifying his complex reasons because he realizes all too well her inability to understand their meaning. That he has been faced with a very real temptation is made clear by his avowal that "all of me wants to," but her failure to understand his renunciation makes his rejection of her proposal all the more appropriate.

Brigid's total insufficiency as a partner for Sam Spade is made even clearer by her question, "Would you have done this

[127]

to me if the falcon had been real and you had been paid your money?" His answer, as he puts it, "Don't be too sure I'm as crooked as I'm supposed to be. That kind of reputation might be good business. . . ."[85] This is entirely consistent with his role playing throughout; moreover, nowhere in the novel has greed been shown to be a characteristic of his. He could have easily taken and kept the thousand dollars Gutman gave him, and he could have gone away with Brigid. Returning Gutman's money and turning in Brigid make speculation concerning Spade's possible corruption at the end patently absurd.

To see the plot action as I have described it validates, I believe, the hypothesis that Hammett's intention is to effect admiration for Spade's renunciation of Brigid.[86] The close of the novel stresses the terrible price he has to pay for his moral and ethical stand. He has reaffirmed his right to say to Effie: "Your Sam's a detective." His code is real, strict, even cruel in its purity; but her response indicates the difference between them: "'You're right. But don't touch me now—not now.' Spade's face became pale as his collar."[87] Effie, too, cannot thoroughly understand Spade's singleness of vision and strict adherence to his own private code. Though he may be right, even heroically right, he is an outsider nevertheless. He lost Brigid, as he had to, and now Effie is lost to him, at least temporarily. In our last sight of him we see him shiver before Iva comes into his office, a reaction that suggests that he feels for the first time his existential loneliness.

There is little optimism in *The Maltese Falcon*, but there is hope. There is, I believe, an integrated moral vision presented, but it stresses the price man must pay to be an authentic self in a corrupt world. In world where all else seems problematic and deceptive, Spade's integrity provides a basis for action in an immoral and amoral universe. His job has clarity: like the plot itself, the job provides a beginning, middle, and an end and thus becomes a way to hold on to one's own reality. Caught between inept and corrupt law enforcement, on the one hand, and the criminal world on the other, he is by his very profession an outsider. He is, as one critic puts it, "most intensely the denizen of the dark borderland between good and evil."[88] If we are to judge Hammett's success as an artist, we must see his work as being not a detective story, but a story about a detective. Kenney has argued that Hammett fails to persuade the reader that what the novel relates pertains to human experience as we know it,[89] but Kenney misses several points.

First, Hammett has in fact created a recognizable human underworld, and has created a believable hero to act in it. Though the villains are strange and exotic, their motivations for acting are all too familiar. Their rapacious competitiveness and greed make them recognizable emblems of American society in the 1920s and 1930s. Hammett's emphasis is not on their exoticism but on their all too common depravity.

Secondly, Hammett's rendering of the action in the novel points to issues much larger than itself. Spade's conception of reality, both as it is reflected in the Flitcraft parable and in his own actions, finds it progenitor in Hamlet's "the readiness is all," and seems almost prophetic of the modern recognition that external supports such as the old American myths of innocence and invincibility are as empty of value or as unreal as the Maltese falcon, and as misleading. In Hammett's world, the authentic man, whoever he might be, lives in a dangerously open and dynamic environment, a place of violent and irrational human behavior where law and formula do not apply.[90] He is essentially an outsider, an exile, from his community even though his job is to search out corruption and attempt to right injustice.

Thirdly, Hammett's fictional world mirrors his own reality. He writes about Spade:

He is a dream man in the sense that he is what most of the private detectives I worked with would like to have been and what quite a few of them in their cockier moments thought they approached. For your private detective does not—or did not ten years ago when he was my colleague—want to be an erudite solver of riddles in the Sherlock Holmes manner; he wants to be a hard and shifty fellow, able to take care of himself in any situation, able to get the best of anybody he comes in contact with, whether criminal, innocent by-stander or client.[91]

External evidence supports my argument that Hammett intended his readers to see Spade as triumphantly moral at the end of the novel. Spade's manner is similar to Hammett's own manner of acting in his real life. In the novel, Spade risks life and rejects luxury for the right to do his job as he sees it. Hammett went to jail for his beliefs. The courage Spade shows reflects the courage shown by Hammett's actions. His daughter Jo wrote that Hammett's boss in his early days as a Pinkerton's detective was James Wright, and how "From Wright he absorbed the basics of private investigation, as well as a personal code of honor that would stay with him for the rest of his life."[92] Dignity, loyalty, courage, honor, and a clear-eyed view of one's world—these are characteristics shared by Hammett and his fictional creation Sam Spade. Both suggest the existential assertion that a world without personal evaluation is one without meaning.[93]

The achievement of *The Maltese Falcon* is clear. Hammett's earlier experimentation with women characters—first Dinah, then Gabrielle—find maturity in Brigid. He has done what Chandler felt was impossible: introduced love interest into a mystery and made it work. Spade's detective work discovers not only a murderess but a truth about personal relationships and the nature of human reality.

For the first time Hammett has created a fully realized hero and has been able to conceptualize an answer to his most vexing question in the first two novels: can a moral man act in a corrupt world without himself becoming infected? The answer is yes, although the price—skepticism and alienation—is high.

Lastly, Hammett has managed to construct a complex yet moving plot whose parts work together to produce the desired effect. In the dark and nightmarish world of *The Maltese Falcon*, Spade's renunciation is an affirmation of man's remaining vestiges of strength and dignity. The novel is depressing in the usual Hammett sense: the world stays the same. But in the figure of Sam Spade, Hammett crystallizes the notion that somehow human dignity and integrity have survived.

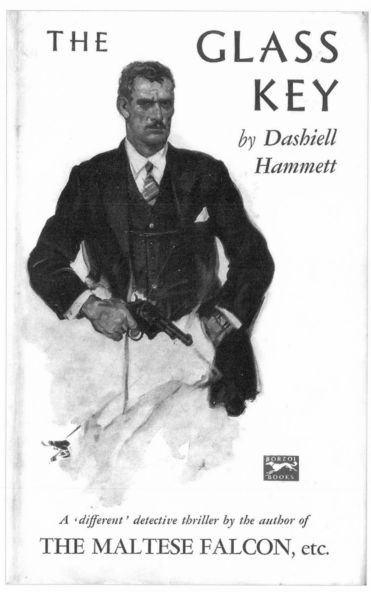

THE GLASS KEY

by Dashiell Hammett

A 'different' detective thriller by the author of
THE MALTESE FALCON, etc.

The Glass Key *was first published in London, England on January 20,
1931. Only three copies in dust jackets are known to exist today. They are
worth $90,000 to $120,000 each. Photo courtesy of Mark Sutcliffe.*

CHAPTER SIX

The Glass Key:
The Darkening Vision

C RITICAL RECEPTION OF HAMMETT'S fourth novel, *The*
Glass Key (1931), has always been extremely varied. Hammett said it was better than *The Dain Curse* and *The Maltese
Falcon* because "the clues were nicely placed there, although
nobody seemed to see them,"[1] but David Bazelon argues that
although *The Glass Key* represents Hammett's attempt at a
genuine novel, finally it fails because "We never know whether
Beaumont's motive in solving the murder is loyalty, job-doing,
or love."[2] Bazelon's point seems to be that since there are a
number of possible motives Ned Beaumont might be acting
upon, he is essentially an ambiguous and more complex figure
than his predecessors.

This is an interesting argument because Robert Edenbaum uses precisely the same reasoning to conclude that *The Glass Key* is "the least satisfactory novel" Hammett produced. He claims that Ned Beaumont's motivation for taking the beatings is never clear, and that the "Hammett mask is never lifted" so we cannot ever discover those feelings. He then goes on to say that actions in the novel are determined "mechanistically and animalistically," and that voluntary "mutilation of life...is the subject matter of these novels."[3] He uses the beating scene in Chapter IV to support his view that Beaumont's actions and reactions are mechanistic and instinctual, but this example is hardly fair. Beaten into insensibility, Beaumont can hardly be expected to catalogue his motivations. The novel does, I will argue, make clear why Beaumont refuses to talk to Shad O'Rory or O'Rory's thugs after Beaumont learns the information he needs.

Ben Ray Redman uses Hammett to represent the beginnings of the fall of the mystery story. Seeing in *The Glass Key* and *The Thin Man* only sadism and heroic drinking,[4] Redman misses among other things Beaumont's true feelings toward Paul Madvig , "Mom" Madvig, Opal Madvig, and Janet Henry.

Philip Durham argues that Ned Beaumont comes "The closest to being an amoral character of the kind which was developing in the hardboiled tradition,"[5] a view that stems from his belief that Beaumont is almost inhuman:

[134]

> Other than for certain loyalties, his motions are mechanical and his emotions were not there. He had a smooth manner and some refinement, but what he did or how seemed not to matter.[6]

As in the discovery scene of *The Maltese Falcon*, I think that such misreading comes from a failure to attend to the nuances of Hammett's diction. Matters of feeling and passion are always treated obliquely by Hammett, but that does not mean they do not exist. Part of the power in Hammett's fiction lies in its suggestion that society wreaks such havoc on the moral individual that in order to survive he must develop a new skin, one that can be hard and resilient enough to resist all kinds of assault from the outside. The bleakness of Hammett's vision then may lie not so much that his protagonists are empty or mechanical but in the fact that within his heroes lie great depths of feeling which cannot find expression in the modern world of America. In Sam Spade's case, the only way he could sustain his authentic self was by turning inward, to protect himself behind toughened walls of skepticism and sardonic humor.

Raymond Chandler captures Hammett's sense of the modern world when he writes:

> The realist in murder writes of a world in which gangsters can rule nations and almost rule cities,...where no man can walk down a dark street in safety because law and order are things we talk about but refrain from practicing;...It is not a fragrant world, but it is the world you live in, and certain writers with tough minds and a cool spirit of detachment can make very interesting and even amusing patterns out of it.[7]

[135]

Twenty-five years later Charles Reich comments that so far as the deep ills of industrialized, urban America are concerned, "The remarkable novels of Raymond Chandler, James M. Cain, and Dashiell Hammett come closer to the truth than almost anything else in literature or the social sciences."[8]

The Glass Key portrays a decadent society as fully as *Red Harvest* and has for its hero a man badly scarred, sickened by the world around him. For all his lucidity, Raymond Chandler failed to see that in 1931 Hammett had already accomplished what Chandler said he hoped would someday be done:

> I am not satisfied that. . . sometime, somewhere, perhaps not now nor by me, a novel cannot be written which, ostensibly a mystery and keeping the spice of mystery, will actually be a novel of character and atmosphere with an overtone of violence and fear.[9]

The Maltese Falcon and *The Glass Key* both come close to this description. Chandler himself remarked that "in *The Glass Key* the reader is constantly reminded that the question is who killed Taylor Henry," and the effect obtained is one of "an effect of movement, intrigue, cross-purposes, and the gradual elucidation of character, which is all the detective story has any right to be about anyway."[10]

There is, then, considerable disagreement concerning the novel's worth. It has been called Hammett's best, Hammett's worst; and the critical estimates of Ned Beaumont range from amoral to a genuine and complex human creation. A close examination of the novel reveals, I believe, a growing pessimism in Hammett's view of modern society, and a clear-eyed view of the dilemmas of a man of integrity in an immoral universe.

Having completed *The Maltese Falcon* and having examined the problem of love and betrayal in the characters of Sam and Brigid, Hammett turns to a slightly different theme— friendship and betrayal—and employs a similar pattern of plot development. Ned Beaumont, the best friend of political boss Paul Madvig, sets out to prove Madvig innocent of the charge of having murdered Taylor Henry, the son of Senator Ralph Bancroft Henry.

Beaumont is not a detective, and as such he is a new figure in Hammett's novels. Noting that in Hammett's last novel, *The Thin Man*, the protagonist is only an ex-detective, and that here he is not (officially) a detective at all suggests an interesting possibility—that Hammett created his ideal detective, Sam Spade, and then moved on to examine other, more flawed types of protagonists. It's almost as if by affirming his own authenticity, Spade destroys his effectiveness in the detecting profession. He certainly can no longer sustain the illusion that he is a shadowy figure of possible corruption, so useful in his business. He would be known as the man who turned in the woman he loved rather than sacrifice his principles. Ironically, then, Hammett creates a plot in which the hardboiled hero, in affirming his professional and moral identity, becomes too different from the rest of his world to ever be effective again.

Ned Beaumont, then, is the new figure, a citizen who finds himself playing the detective role to save a friend because no one else can or will. At every turn he meets resistance and lies, but Hammett shows him persevering in spite of beatings and red herrings to accomplish his goal. Ned Beaumont proves Paul Madvig innocent of Taylor Henry's murder, but on so doing discovers his friend to be corrupt in an equally serious sense: for political advantage Madvig was willing to sacrifice Beaumont's friendship and trust. As in *The Maltese Falcon*, detection leads to more than a solution of a mystery: it leads to the discovery of fundamental truths of human reality in a decaying and immoral society.

William Kenney argues that

> Hammett's strategy is to show the process of detection as motivated by and affecting a friendship between two men. One of the ironies lending complexity to the plot is that Madvig, for whose sake the investigation has been undertaken, is trying to stop it for reasons

[137]

of his own. Out of these materials Hammett creates a dynamic structure of uncertain, constantly shifting human relationships.[11]

Kenney regards *The Glass Key* as the one Hammett work that comes the "closest to achieving the ideal of the modern detective novel"[12] because it possesses a dynamic plot structure and represents "Hammett's most ambitious study of moral ambiguity."[13]

I would rather say that it renders more concretely than any of Hammett's other novels the attempt of the hero to get outside of himself by acting on what is best within himself for someone else, only to find, painfully, that the attempt merely proves the impossibility of such behavior.

Hammett's choice of protagonist and creation of a particular milieu for him to act in suggest his expanding moral and social vision. One of the premises of this study is that Hammett experimented with his materials to portray the human dilemmas of modern man. To a large extent, *The Glass Key* is a composite of *Red Harvest* and *The Maltese Falcon*, attempting to combine the social emphasis of the earlier work with the more moral and personal stress of the later book. Beaumont resembles the

Continental Op in his immersion in the corrupt world around him, his recognition that he shares in its decadence, and in his ability to understand political realities and know how they can be used more effectively. He most resembles Sam Spade in his adherence to a code of personal ethics and in his desire to have a meaningful human relationship.

Although Hammett shows society's social and moral corruption in his previous novels, nowhere does he make the portrait so extensive and believable as he does in *The Glass Key*. Corruption pervades all levels, as it does in his earlier works, but here the representatives and symbols of that fact are more personalized and more functionally connected in the plot. The novel opens on a note of political expediency:

> "You know damned well I can't help it, Ned. With everybody up for re-election and the women's clubs on the war-path it would be jumping in the lake to have Tim's case squared now."[14]

Tim Ivans is in jail. His brother Walt Ivans wants him out now, but Paul Madvig makes it clear that the time is not right. Two points are made here: one, that during normal times Madvig is powerful enough to get someone out of jail, and two, in times of political crisis a man, even presumed innocent, must remain in jail until the crisis passes. In both cases, law and justice play no part in affecting decisions made. Squaring a man's case *seems* to be a matter of political priorities, not a matter of the man's innocence or guilt.

Though Madvig's central concern seems to be expediency, we see that his notion of what is expedient differs considerably from Beaumont's. Hammett emphasizes the falseness and inner sickness of the society in *The Glass Key* by showing that even the most powerful of men, Paul Madvig, is incapable of seeing beyond his own self-interest. He is a Machiavellian *manqué*, one who talks about being a political realist while his actions reveal just how un-pragmatic he really is. When, for example, Beaumont tells Madvig to throw over Senator Henry because the Senator cannot be trusted, Madvig refuses. When pushed by Beaumont to defend his position, Madvig admits that his agreement with Senator Henry rests on the assumption that Janet Henry, the Senator's daughter, will marry him if the Senator wins reelection. Beaumont sees how foolish that assumption is. As he says, Senator Henry is an aristocrat,

"And his daughter's an aristocrat. That's why I'm warning you to sew your shirt on when you go to see them, or you'll come away without it, because to them you're a lower form of animal life and none of the rules apply."[15]

Beaumont sees the class distinction and doubts that Madvig's romantic hopes have any chance of eventual success. William Kenney makes a good point when he argues that Paul Madvig

has allowed his desire for a woman and for a kind of respectability...to lead him to deceive his closest friends and to weaken the professional judgment that has made him an effective political boss.[16]

Hammett makes this clear in this scene that Madvig's "political" considerations are really personal ones that run counter to sound political thinking. Beaumont's cynical comment "We didn't have to do much worrying about women's clubs before we joined the aristocracy" and his warning to Madvig that keeping Tim Ivans in jail may cause considerable unrest among his own backers ("You know it won't take a lot of this to start them saying it was different in the old days before you put in with the Senator.") both point to Madvig's inability to understand the world he lives in. [17]

In fact, Madvig's self-centered view of reality is shown to be the cause of great anguish to those closest to him. With his desire to win the hand of Janet, Madvig arbitrarily forbids his daughter Opal to see Senator Henry's son, Taylor Henry, because Madvig knows the Senator disapproves. This political-personal decision forces Opal Madvig to see Taylor Henry secretly. Later Paul Madvig further contributes to Opal's nervous strain by allowing her to think he, Madvig, is guilty of her lover Taylor's murder, thus forcing her to turn against her own father, to go to newspaper publisher Hal Mathews with what she thinks is proof of Madvig's guilt, and eventually to attempt suicide. A victim of her father's selfishness, Opal reminds us of Ophelia in *Hamlet* who also discovered that her mind was unable to cope with extreme contradictions.

Madvig's concern for himself affects Ned Beaumont as well. Madvig is willing to encourage Beaumont to believe he is guilty of Taylor Henry's murder and to let Beaumont endure horrific beatings in his search for the truth about the death of Taylor Henry because Madvig thinks that with Senator Henry's support Madvig can win the election and marry the Senator's daughter, Janet. Madvig uses Beaumont's loyalty and trust to further his own political and personal interests, thus making a mockery of Beaumont's sacrifices.

Janet Henry is another victim of Paul Madvig's political corruption. Forced by her senator father to pretend to accept Madvig's affection, she finds herself having to pursue the unpleasant task of trying to prove Madvig guilty of murder in order to avoid him. Janet Henry clearly perceives that her father is not going to demand the murderer be found until after the election, and she suspects he is purposely covering up for Madvig to gain reelection. By the end, she is confronted with the fact that her own father killed her brother and ". . . let him lie there, like that, in the street!"[18] all for political reasons.

By making the struggles of Opal Madvig and Janet Henry integral parts of his plot, Hammett renders poignantly the human predicament with its attendant pain. His society is a coldly political one, where human lives are used and forgotten in larger games of manipulation and control.

There is an additional irony: Though children suffer the sins of their parents, the elders themselves are trapped in their own game. The helplessness of even the most powerful of men is emphasized by Hammett's portrayals of Senator Henry, District Attorney Michael Joseph Farr, newspaper publisher Hal Mathews, political boss Paul Madvig, several policemen, and detective Jack Rumsen. All but Beaumont are enslaved, in one way or another. Senator Henry's fear and insecurity concerning his ability to win re-election without Madvig's support, for example, forces him to commit murder and forsake all responsibility for his daughter. The obsession to cling to his precarious position of power drives him relentlessly; his will to power is totally destructive. Empty-hearted and ruled by fear, Senator Henry is a symbol of the new legislator in the new status civilization.

District Attorney Farr, likewise, represents the new breed of law enforcement personnel. For all the power of his office, he too is helpless, dependent on the political winds to dictate his moves. Rather than being an enforcer of the law, he is a parasite on the political system, one of the "pimps" Beaumont so hates. When, for example, Farr receives one of the mysterious notes obliquely accusing Paul Madvig of Taylor's murder, Beaumont tells him to ignore it and not to bother Madvig about it: "I don't think I'd say anything to him about it if I were you. He's got enough on his mind." Despite the second murder in the novel—Francis West's—which also seems to be the work of Paul Madvig's people, Farr never moves against him. As he says to Beaumont: "You know damned well there's nobody in the city any stronger for Paul and for you than me...you can always count on me." Farr is uninterested in solving Taylor Henry's murder until the political wind shifts away from Paul Madvig. [19]

The town's major newspaper, *The Observer*, is run by Hal Mathews. Instead of its being a powerful source of truth, it is simply a political football. Mathews is another helpless figure of power:

"Mathews is up to his ears in debt. The State Central
Trust Company holds both mortgages on his plants—
one on his house, too, for that matter. The State Central belongs to Bill Roan. Bill Roan is running for the
Senate against Henry. Mathews does what he's told to
do and prints what he's told to print."[20]

Because his financial life is controlled by others, Mathews
is trapped. Beaumont tells us that Mathews does not believe
Madvig murdered Taylor Henry, but he has no freedom or
power to disagree with those who want Madvig found guilty.

It is the feeling of revulsion stemming from the recognition
of Mathews' weak and impotent nature that pushes Mathews'
wife into a betrayal with Beaumont. The "gray-faced man who
shivered before the look in his wife's eyes"[21] comes downstairs in
the middle of the night and witnesses a kissing scene between
Beaumont and Eloise, his wife. Knowing he has betrayed her
in a far more fundamental way, Mathews retreats back upstairs,
enters his room and shoots himself. This suicide, like Senator
Henry's plea for a revolver at the end,[22] suggest the utter impotency and essential loneliness of this new breed of men, the kind
of men Charles A. Reich describes in *The Greening of America*:

[143]

Man became alienated from himself as money, not
inner needs, called the tune. Man began to defer or
abandon his real needs, and increasingly his wants
became subjects to outward manipulation.[23]

Such men are committed to nothing within themselves, engage
with nothing that relates to themselves, and are therefore
manipulated wholly by external stimuli.

As we have already seen, despite all of Paul Madvig's
political leverage, he, too, is a figure of the same unreality and

impotence. The novel makes it quite clear that without Ned Beaumont's advice Paul Madvig would not long hold his power. Madvig constantly seeks Beaumont's thoughts on political and personal matters, and he seems overall a man not quite aware of his times. Madvig lets his anger dictate his moves against Shad O'Rory—he wants a gang war—and is willing to betray Ned Beaumont, his only solid friend, in the hope of satisfying his longing for Janet Henry and the respectability she represents. In a particular way Madvig plays the "sap" part that Sam Spade refused to play in *The Maltese Falcon* and that Beaumont warns against in this novel. We like Madvig better than some of the other characters because he seems human, but his corruption is the corruption of the spirit. Like many other characters in the novel, Paul Madvig's priorities are perverted. In the closing scene of the novel he is reminiscent of Henry James' protagonist in "The Beast in the Jungle." Like James' story of John Marcher, Paul Madvig's story illustrates the failure of being fully alive. Having led a life of selfish delusion, he loses what could have been most valuable. By the end of the novel, Madvig stands helplessly by while Beaumont accuses him of being largely responsible for his daughter Opal's nervous breakdown—"You did it to her"—and shows Madvig that the political organization he built was rooted in sand: "What are you going to do with your not quite faithful henchmen? Kick them back in line?"[24] Madvig's response suggests he may have learned something:

> "I'm going to teach them something. . . . It'll cost me four years, but I can use these four years cleaning house and putting together an organization that will stay put."[25]

But he learns at a great price: his only friend leaves him. His plea—"Have you got to go, Ned?"—is answered by Beaumont's

"Got to," and his anguished retort, "Well, it serves me right," sums up the note of poetic justice on which then novel closes. [26]

The police are all on the take, sometimes from Madvig, sometimes from Shad O'Rory, and sometimes from both at the same time. They too are not their own men. As Madvig tells Beaumont, the police owe him "debts" that will take them a good while to pay off.[27] It is not surprising that the dominant imagery of the novel is business imagery. It is largely about the buying and selling of loyalties, and the police are as bought as everyone else. Those whom Madvig can't reach, O'Rory reaches: "I mean that half the coppers in the town are buying their cakes and ale with dough they're getting from me and some of my friends."[28] Perhaps the best example of legal impotence after District Attorney Farr is Beaumont's detective helper, Jack Rumsen. When Beaumont pretends he is after Madvig's scalp for Taylor Henry's murder, he asks Rumsen to help him, but Rumsen refuses:

> "Fred and I are building up a nice little private-detective business here. . . A couple of years more and we'll be sitting pretty. I like you, Beaumont, but not enough to monkey with the man that runs the city."[29]

[145]

Again business concerns weigh more heavily than the pursuit of truth or professional pride. In his clear-eyed view that he is a small cog within a large system, detective Jack Rumsen represents the powerlessness of modern man and the death of the private eye.

It is fitting, therefore, that Hammett chooses for the hero of *The Glass Key* an amateur detective. The implication is that the last outpost of moral strength and individuality within the legal system—the private eye—is gone, subsumed by the larger, more powerful organization. Where once the cop was expected to assume the burden of failed or indifferent institutions, and then the private eye, now even those last resorts are gone. Jack Rumsen as private eye is a diminished figure of heroic irony. He is the dried-up residue of Natty Bumppo, who kept his "moral integrity hard and intact,"[30] and Sam Spade, who retained his authenticity of self even while losing everything else. Rumsen's timid rigidity is the real image of a modern police force and the course of its omnipresent corruption[31] The only possible figure left is one who is not trapped by the system and who is strong enough to do what no one else can or will do—search for truth.

Dashiell Hammett's creation Ned Beaumont is a work of subtlety and imagination. Beaumont is, first of all, an active participant in the corruption Hammett's novel exposes. He is not an outsider like the Continental Op in *The Dain Curse* or Sam Spade in *The Maltese Falcon*, nor is he a newcomer to the scene, as is the Op in *Red Harvest*. Although he has only been with Paul Madvig's organization fifteen months, he is to a great extent the brains behind the power boss Madvig. Furthermore, he is portrayed as a man of certain weaknesses, not the least of which is his obsession with gambling. Unlike the preceding novels, the initial crime—the murder of Taylor Henry—does not lead the protagonist deeper and deeper into the possibilities of personal corruption; rather, the event gives the protagonist the impetus to adhere to the more positive aspects of his character. *The Maltese Falcon* affords Spade a similar opportunity, as he must weigh the temptations of Brigid against his own sense of self-definition and reality, but *The Maltese Falcon* ends on a much more positive note than *The Glass Key*. By the end, Beaumont is more the shattered hero than Sam Spade, and Beaumont's actions and discoveries measure the distance Hammett has moved towards a pessimistic vision of man's possibilities.

Critics tell us that Beaumont is inhuman and amoral, or that he is finally an enigma of motivation and character. Though I agree that Hammett creates an ambiguity about Beaumont's exact feelings, I think he intends us to see him finally as a sensitive and honorable figure. Again, attention to the nuances of Hammett's diction, and an ability to surmise intention from what is not said but merely implied, is necessary if we are to see into Ned Beaumont's character with any clarity.

Edenbaum and others are quite right in arguing that Hammett does not allow us inside Beaumont's mind. David Bazelon's point is that because Hammett's private eyes have no private life they are therefore too "disinterested" and not real:

> The *moral* problem—the matter of individual respon-
> sibility of decision-making in a situation where society
> has defaulted morally—is never even faced, much less
> solved.[32]

But it seems to me that moral problems *are* faced by Hammett's protagonists, and that the lack of internal monologue may, in fact, be an indication of what Hammett felt fiction should do. In the real world we only know each other by indirect signs, so we never know certainty. So it is with Hammett's characters. Furthermore, his protagonists are detectives (or their equivalent), and they are evaluated in the public eye only by what they *do*, and by this we judge them. It may be that what Edenbaum means when he talks about "the voluntary mutilation of life"[33] as being the subject of Hammett's fiction is that society, being what it is, needs men who can repress their individual feelings in the service of searching out the truth and combating the malaise of corruption that pervades man's institutions. In this sense, the men who do this become victims of the society that creates the job, and this is one of the major themes of *The Glass Key*.

Hammett's refusal to show a character's inner thoughts except by indirection may indicate that he feels realistic fiction should reflect the shattered and inarticulate state of man. If Hammett in fact can, through stylistic nuance, render such a meaning, then he is successful. If not, then only confusion reigns.

Before turning to examples showing where I think Hammett is successful in such indirection, we will examine carefully the way in which he has arranged his plot. It is my contention that Hammett's ordering of events implies a good deal about Ned Beaumont's inner nature.

Early in the novel, for example, Beaumont chases a bookie, Bernie Despain, to New York City. He goes for two reasons. First, there is a possibility that Despain is connected with the murder of Taylor Henry:, and if so, then Ned can immediately prove his friend Paul Madvig innocent. But at this point in the action Beaumont's overriding reason is personal. A habitual loser at gambling, Beaumont for once has won three thousand two hundred and fifty dollars, and to lose it all now to a welsher would be more than he can stand:

> "I've got to get this guy. I've got to.". . . "Listen Paul: it's not only the money, though thirty-two hundred is a lot, but it would be the same if it was five bucks. I go two months without winning a bet and that gets me down. What good am I if my luck's gone? Then I cop, or think I do, and I'm all right again. I can take my tail from between my legs and feel that I'm a person again and not just something that's being kicked around. The money's important enough, but it's not the real thing. It's what losing and losing and losing does to me. Can you get that? It's getting me licked. And then, when I think I've worn out the jinx, this guy takes a Mickey Finn on me. I can't stand for it. If I stand for it I'm

licked, my nerve's gone. I'm not going to stand for it. I'm going after him."[34]

These lines reveal a great deal more about Beaumont than might first appear. They give us an insight into the nature and quality of his life up to this point. They imply that his life is relatively empty of meaning; obviously Paul Madvig's success, and any hand Beaumont may have had in it, carry no real meaning for him. He seems little better off than he was before Madvig picked him "up out of the gutter."[35] His identity is measured only by his gain or loss in the gambler's throw of the dice. At this juncture, he must collect his winnings or his nerve will fail him. These lines present us with the image of a man who evaluates himself solely in terms of winning or losing on the wings of Lady Luck; he is otherwise empty and devoid of purpose. In a very real personal sense he is the epitome of a loser.

Beaumont has only one outstanding quality at this point: guts. Though shaken by bad luck, he will not stand for being played as a sap. He will resist as long as he can. Unlike Hammett's earlier heroes, he is a physically weak man. A hard drinker, and tubercular as well,[36] he nevertheless traces Despain down and, though beaten repeatedly by Despain's thug, he uses his intelligence and puts the squeeze on Despain to get his money.

The reason Hammett selects these scenes to open *The Glass Key* is two-fold: on the one hand, to give us a sense of the emptiness of Beaumont's life to this point, and on the other, to indicate that underneath it all lays an untapped reservoir of strength and determination. Ned Beaumont will not be a loser again if he can help it, and he believes in Paul Madvig. The main action of the novel provides an opportunity for this inner strength to find direction and purpose. The murder of Taylor Henry is the stimulus, and as Madvig increasingly appears to be threatened with a murder charge, Beaumont's life takes on added strength of purpose and dimension: to prove Madvig innocent. Hammett's plot is arranged in such a way as to show the growth of Beaumont. To some degree the novel is a novel of "becoming," with the tragic irony that once you come into being you are so unlike everyone else in your world that you are a permanent outsider.

Critics have talked about Beaumont's hardness, but no one has commented on his compassion. Hammett gives an early example of it when he describes Beaumont's meeting with Opal Madvig after her lover Taylor Henry has been murdered. Underneath Beaumont's hardboiled public role is sympathy: "His eyes were humid with sympathy. His voice husky. 'I know, youngster, it's tough.'" He tries to talk about Taylor, but Opal lies to him, saying she hasn't seen him in months. Ned responds, "'You oughtn't to lie to me,' he said gravely as he sat down." To her question, "Aren't we friends?" he says: "Sure,... but it's hard to remember it when we're lying to each other.'"[37]

These are crucial lines for an understanding of Beaumont's character as well as for the plot of the entire novel. His point is that friendship and lies cannot coexist, that trust is a necessary ingredient of a human relationship. This is a moral perception, a perception based on a standard of value. This emphasis on trust is an integral part of his nature; throughout the novel he exhibits trust in Madvig's innocence, and expects to be trusted in return. This is why the revelations at the end so shatter him.

[150]

Beaumont makes this same plea for trust to Madvig's mother in Chapter V. The Madvigs are the only "family" Beaumont seems to have, and when he goes to see her and she asks him if her son Paul killed Taylor Henry, Hammett gives us this description of Beaumont's reaction:

> Merriment went out of his eyes and voice. "He didn't
> do it, Mom." He smiled at her. He smiled with his lips

only and they were thin against his teeth. "It would be nice if somebody in town besides me thought he didn't do it and it would be especially nice if that other one was his mother."[38]

As the thin lips against the teeth imply, Beaumont is furious at her lack of trust in her son, but he admonishes her though understatement only. Hammett emphasizes Beaumont's continuing faith in his friend and his strong sense that the basis of human relationships ought to be trust.

The characteristics we have uncovered in Beaumont's nature are clarified, developed, tested, and finally shattered by the main action. J. Ross-McLaren's statement concerning Beaumont's behavior in the novel is more accurate than most:

> We believe as implicitly in Beaumont's selfless devotion to Madvig as Beaumont himself believes in his friend's innocence of murder, despite all the evidence to the contrary.[39]

A continuing problem for some critics, the question of Beaumont's motivation, is made quite clear, I believe, not by what he says, so much, as by what he does. Action defines Hammett's characters, and the actions Beaumont take increasingly reveal that his motivation is loyalty to the man he trusts. In the opening chapters, I have argued, Beaumont's actions are essentially self-centered. Until the murder of Francis West and the appearance of the first of the mysterious letters suggesting Paul Madvig's guilt, the issue of Madvig's innocence or guilt is not potent. But with these new developments, Beaumont's world becomes Madvig-centered. Is Madvig guilty? And can Madvig hold power in a situation in which everyone seems bent on bringing him down? As Beaumont describes the problem to Madvig:

"Well, everybody, or a lot of them, is going to start won-
dering whether you didn't have the witnesses against his
brother shot and frightened into silence. That goes for
the outsiders, the women's clubs you're getting so afraid
of these days, and the respectable citizens. The insid-
ers—the ones that mostly wouldn't care if you had done
that—are going to get something like the real news.
They're going to know that one of your boys had to go
to Shad to get fixed up and that Shad fixed him up."[40]

The Francis West murder is an important element in the plot
because it puts Madvig in a vulnerable position *vis a vis* public
opinion and his own political position within his own organization. Though Beaumont does not know who killed West, he
accurately surmises that O'Rory is responsible.

The most immediate problem, then, is an upcoming battle
for control of the city. This Beaumont sees clearly, just as he
sees that to fight it out in the streets is pointless. As he tells
Madvig, Shad O'Rory will fight back, and the consequences
will destroy Madvig's power:

"You're trying to re-elect the whole city administration.
Well, giving them a crime-wave—and one it's an even
bet they're not going to be able to handle—just before
the election isn't going to make them look any too
efficient."[41]

The only way Beaumont can stop Madvig from being foolish
is to put himself on the line. He refuses to back down in front
of Madvig:

". . . I do think you've let yourself be outsmarted this
time. First you let the Henrys wheedle you into backing

the Senator. That was your chance to go in and finish
an enemy who was cornered, but that enemy happened
to have a daughter and social position and what not, so
you—"[42]

Beaumont exercises the kind of guts we saw in the Despain
episode; he is willing to quit his job and go to New York. Again
we sense his determination not to be a loser. When Madvig hits
him, Beaumont calls him a fool and leaves. The split seems
irrevocable until Madvig capitulates, and calls him back.

In many ways Beaumont is reminiscent of the Machiavellian
advisor in his ability to improvise and manipulate. It is interesting to speculate whether or not he purposely chose to do battle
with Madvig at that particular time and place in order to gain
entrance into Shad O'Rory's gang. Hammett gives us no clear-
cut indication either way, but we do know that Beaumont goes to
O'Rory in order to set a trap for O'Rory: "I went there to lay a trap
for the gent and he out-trapped me."[43] And we know that word of
their fight spread all over town, thus providing Beaumont with
his opportunity. We also know that Beaumont was testing Paul
Madvig to see if Madvig would lose his head in a fight.[44]

In any case, O'Rory offers Beaumont a proposition: come
across with enough dirt to ruin Madvig and he can have the
finest gambling house in the state. In the beginning of the
novel, such an offer might have been enough to seduce Beaumont, but here it proves to have no effect because, as I intend to
show, he has found a more meaningful purpose in life: protect-
ing Paul Madvig. Throughout the meeting, Beaumont is in full
control: he masks his feelings and plays the malcontent role.
His purpose is to find the truth concerning the West murder,
and he does: O'Rory arranged it. When Beaumont tries to
leave, O'Rory's henchmen beat him into insensibility and lock
him in a room.

The scenes which follow are incredibly brutal and savage, and it is here that critics have problems. Why, they ask, does he take the beatings instead of giving them the information? Why endure the pain? Edenbaum argues we cannot tell: it may be out of loyalty, but it may have nothing to do with loyalty:

> It can be argued, on the contrary, that Ned takes the beatings, not out of loyalty but out of indifference to death (to falling beams, if you will). He "can stand anything [he's] got to stand," a gangster's sadism no more and no less than his (apparent) tuberculosis...But "standing" punishment stoically (or suicidally) is not loyalty, not a basis for positive action; and without some clarification of motive, the sense of Ned's activities is merely muddy.[45]

A man who stoically stands punishment simply for the sake of standing punishment is one who has nothing else to live for. This seems to be Edenbaum's point, but I do not think the situation is this simple.

William F. Nolan goes even further by suggesting that we cannot even be sure of Beaumont's honesty:

> Did he suffer this agony out of loyalty to his friend or because his ego was threatened? Would he have walked out with O'Rory's money and laughed about it with Madvig, or would he have sent O'Rory the damaging information he wanted? Or is Beaumont really "a damned massacrist" as Jeff calls him? We don't know. Hammett does not tell us.[46]

Both critics raise the same important issue: how can we know Ned Beaumont's motivations during the scene? The answer is we cannot. Hammett refuses to let the reader into the mind of his protagonist, and thus he makes immediate judgments difficult, if not impossible. By keeping the reader off-center, Hammett creates a variety of effects. First of all, he intensifies our sense of the problematic nature of reality. Is it loyalty or self-sufficiency or ego that motivates Beaumont? It may be all three or any combination, but not until the following chapter, Chapter V, can we make an accurate determination.

Secondly, Hammett's restraint forces the reader to question his own preconceived assumptions concerning the nature of Beaumont. Up to this point, the reader identifies with Beaumont and likes him; therefore a scene that may suggest the corruptibility of one of the few likeable people in the novel deepens our sense of fear and unease. We hope that it is not so, but fear that it may be. Later, when Hammett shows us it was a false alarm, we feel relief and an increased admiration for the protagonist.

It is my position that by Chapter V we know the answer—it was loyalty—but by making us wait to discover the answer, Hammett has again stressed one of his most dominant themes: the necessity of reappraising human experience. From this point on, Hammett gives us abundant reasons to believe that loyalty was the central, if not the sole, reason for Beaumont's suffering in Chapter IV.

Of course, Beaumont tells us himself that he went to O'Rory's for Madvig's sake, but he might be lying. But if we look closely at Hammett's handling of the hospital scene, we find substantial reasons for believing Beaumont. We are told, for example, that when Beaumont wakes he is informed by Madvig that while unconscious he had blurted out the crucial information about the Francis West killing. Hammett manifests Beaumont's single-minded loyalty to Madvig by showing that even while unconscious he speaks to save him. As well, there is confirming evidence in Janet Henry's words to Beaumont:

"You're his best friend." She paused, then added: "He thinks so."

"What do you think?" he asked with incomplete seriousness.

"I think you are," she said gravely, "or you would not have gone through that for him."[47]

Her words represent what we would normally assume by such an exhibition of endurance, and Beaumont's actions, both conscious and unconscious, support it.

Further, every action Beaumont takes in the novel evinces his willingness to trust in Madvig's innocence. He employs private eye Jack Rumsen to find out who is writing the mysterious letters implicating Madvig in the murder, and he tells Rumsen repeatedly that Madvig is innocent. At the Mathews' house, the first thing he does after discovering Hal Mathews' body is to read his will and then destroy it before it can fall into Shad O'Rory's hands. The will gives the State Central Trust Company (run by Shad's people) complete control of Mathew's paper. Beaumont immediately calls Madvig and tells him to stop the morning edition from hitting the streets because it would be carrying Opal Madvig's fantasies about her father's guilt. Beaumont's mind always concentrates on an *idée fixe*: protect Madvig by finding out who killed Taylor Henry.

When, for example, Beaumont discovers that Janet Henry has been writing the letters accusing Madvig, he sympathizes with her because he understands why she did it, but he continues to argue for Paul Madvig's innocence: "Paul wouldn't have to kill Taylor and he wouldn't've done it." He tells her "You're right about my being Paul's friend. I'm that no matter who he killed," and "The part of you that's tricked Paul and is trying to trick him is my enemy," phrases which hardly reflect disinterest in Madvig's welfare. [48]

Madvig's situation becomes increasingly serious as two new witnesses (Harry Sloss and Ben Ferriss) appear who can place Paul Madvig on the scene of the crime. The election campaign also begins to lose ground and District Attorney Farr begins to turn against Madvig. Beaumont is now convinced he must force Madvig to tell what he knows about the Taylor Henry murder:

> "If Taylor Henry's killing isn't cleared up pronto you won't have to worry about the campaign. You'll be sunk whoever wins."[49]

He sees clearly that Madvig's people are going to cross him if things become too heated, but despite his pleas, Madvig refuses to confide in Beaumont. Instead, Madvig attempts to stop him from pursuing the question of Taylor Henry's murder by confessing that he, Madvig, killed him.[50] He gives his love for Janet Henry as his reason for having kept quiet and, when Beaumont tells him how Janet really feels about him, Madvig fires him.

We later discover that Madvig's confession is a phony, but at this point in the novel we believe Madvig is telling the truth. Our feeling is a mixture of a sense of horror and a sense of anguish for Ned Beaumont who has suffered so much for his belief of Madvig's innocence. Hammett makes us feel that things cannot get any worse, that the ultimate betrayal has taken place, but the ending of the novel shows this assumption to have been an optimistic delusion.

Beaumont's reaction to Madvig's "kiss-off" is to feel sorry but justified: "I'm sorry . . . but I wouldn't have gone a step out of my way to avoid it."[51] Though it appears that Beaumont's trust has been misplaced, and that Madvig is willing to be a loser, Beaumont can still fall back on his adherence to truth. Madvig could not accept the truth about Janet Henry's feelings and he confessed to a crime Beaumont is still sure he didn't commit.

It is Madvig's "revelation" which accounts for Beaumont's most cynical and amoral statement in the novel: "I don't believe in anything, but I'm too much of a gambler not to be affected by a lot of things."[52] Critics use this line to argue that Beaumont possesses a vision of meaninglessness throughout, but that is to fail to see that this quasi-Flitcraftian statement comes almost immediately following the scene with Madvig, and, therefore suggests the bitterness Beaumont feels at this point. He has believed Madvig throughout, and now he has been betrayed. Beaumont's fish dream (which he recounts to Janet Henry on the same page as his statement about not believing in anything) reflects the disappointment he feels:

> "I was fishing," he said, "and I caught an enormous fish—a rainbow trout, but enormous—and you said you wanted to look at it and you picked it up and threw it back in the water before I could stop you."[53]

His dream is one of success—he catches a big fish—but someone else interferes and he loses it. From one perspective this reflects his ongoing fear that he will never be more than a loser. From another, the sense of loss here may be Beaumont's way of expressing the feeling that Janet Henry will end up disappointing him as Paul Madvig has done.

[158]

After Madvig's confession, an interesting scene with Janet occurs. Beaumont seems to believe Madvig's story, but encourages Janet to help him search for confirming evidence. At this point in the novel we are not certain whether Beaumont believes Madvig is guilty or not. All we are sure of is that he knows Janet Henry can be useful if he can convince her to aid him in an impartial investigation for the truth. He needs her to check on two clues: the whereabouts of the walking stick her brother Taylor supposedly carried the night he was killed, and whether or not any hats were missing from her house. Furthermore, by enlisting Janet's help Beaumont keeps her from exposing Madvig's supposed guilt to the authorities until he has followed out his own leads.

Hammett makes it increasingly apparent in the scenes following Madvig's confession that although Beaumont's friendship with Madvig has been compromised, Beaumont continues in his single-minded belief that Madvig is not guilty of Taylor Henry's murder. Although there is irony in the fact that Beaumont's basis for undertaking the investigation in the first place is now gone—friendship—Hammett shows that truth is still important to Beaumont. Hammett elevates his hero by showing him to have greater faith than us; we have already accepted Madvig's guilt. But Beaumont continues his search for the same reason he earlier kept after Bernie Despain: he cannot deny himself. He cannot keep losing and losing; if Madvig is in fact guilty, then Beaumont is again a loser. Loyalty influences his decision, but so does his determination not to be a loser. He must see it through if he is to hold on to anything.

Beaumont goes to Farr's office and gives an affidavit concerning what Madvig told him. This a brilliant move because it puts Madvig's confession in black and white detail so that if Farr finds counter-evidence Madvig's innocence will be unmistakably clear to the public. Further, it forces Farr to pick up [159] Madvig for murder, thus creating the situation where the real murderer will have to reveal himself to prevent Paul from telling the truth. Beaumont then goes to see the thug Jeff Gardner in order to pry information from him about Taylor Henry's murder. As in Janet's first rendition of her dream of the glass key, Beaumont is opening the door to let the snakes out to let them kill each other off: Gardner kills O'Rory because the latter suspects Gardner of betraying him.[54]

In the case of the Senator, Beaumont's squeeze play works perfectly. Apprised by Beaumont that Madvig is to be picked up by Farr, Senator Henry panics and tries to leave his home with a gun with the intention of killing Madvig, thus exposing his own guilt. Janet Henry having found the walking stick in the house and no hats missing provides Beaumont with clear evidence; he now pieces the mystery together, and truth is revealed.

Janet's dream of the glass key is most horribly realized. In her dream she and Beaumont were unable to unlock a door that would allow them to eat the sumptuous food on the table inside. The glass key shattered in their hands, and they had to force the door: "We couldn't lock the snakes in and they came out all over us and I woke screaming."[55] The discovery that her father murdered his own son, her brother, is the terrifying truth, and perhaps it is this horrible reality that the snakes represent in the dream. Janet Henry and Ned Beaumont force the truth to emerge, just as in the dream they force the locked door. In both dream and reality the anticipated result—for Janet, the food and Madvig's guilt—is not reached.

In Beaumont's case, the snakes in the dream mirror the dreadful reality that he discovers: Madvig's betrayal of friendship. Hammett makes it clear towards the end of Chapter IX just how disappointed and hurt Beaumont is over his discovery. "Mom" Madvig asks him if there is anything that can patch up their friendship, and Hammett renders Beaumont's response this way:

> He raised his head and looked at her. His eyes were wet. He said gently: "No Mom, that's done for good."[56]

Hammett does not let us inside Beaumont's mind except by suggestion, but it is clear that Hammett intends us to see deep feeling in Beaumont's heart. Admittedly, the novel would have greater force had Hammett not so underplayed Beaumont's bitterness and sense of betrayal. I think one reason he does so is to be found in Hammett's comment to Lillian Hellman that he hates to talk about such things.[57] He implies that a man's suffering should be a private matter, not to be shared by others. It's the hardboiled idea that talking about it cannot change it, only sentimentalize it. Such an idea seems based on the premise that suffering is a universal fact and that the best a man can do is accept his own lot and deal with it. This may not make for great art, but it certainly makes for an intense personal vision.

The pessimism of Hammett's vision is reflected in Beaumont's fate. He ends with little. Robert Edenbaum suggests that the Ned-Janet relationship is quite problematic. It may be, he asserts, that Madvig's view that Beaumont lied to him earlier about Beaumont's feelings toward Janet may have some substantiality:

> The men have a falling out when Paul accuses Ned of lying to him because of Ned's own interest in Janet; at the end of the novel, Paul is confronted by the couple going off together. The question remains whether Paul was right in the first place, whether Ned acted out of a desire for the girl rather than loyalty to Paul or for neither reason. But here is no basis for judgment, by Janet *or* the reader. Motives are once again indeterminable, but in this book it is necessary that they be determined.[58]

This seems to me to miss the point. What Beaumont tells Madvig is the truth, and the purpose of it is to stop him from playing the "sap" and to tell what he knows about the Taylor Henry murder. The action of the novel makes it clear that Beaumont's motivation is never, with the exception of the Despain affair, self-centered. It is always directed outward, toward Madvig.

The real ambiguity surrounds Beaumont's feelings for Janet. Hammett's first subtle indication that Beaumont may feel something for her is in his revision of the last line of the letter he writes her in Chapter V. Having originally ended it with a split infinitive—"to more clearly show my gratitude"—he rewrites it to read, "to show my gratitude more clearly,"[59] in order to appear

[161]

more refined.[60] Later he joins her in the search for the truth concerning Madvig, a venture he knows will not prove pleasant for her: "I hope you will like it when you get it."[61]

In the final scene with Senator Henry, Beaumont does not try to shield Janet from the emerging truth, and she proves strong enough to take it: "'I don't want to be spared,' she said in a small flat voice. 'I want to know.'"[62] Her strength in this scene makes her a suitable partner for him because both are able to face the truth in a world where everyone else denies it (Paul Madvig), ignores it (Senator Henry), or is crushed by it (Opal Madvig).

Hammett purposely keeps Beaumont's feelings about Janet vague, and for good reason. Too much stress on them would indeed make his motives suspect. Hammett plays down their relationship consistently, right to the end. When Janet asks Beaumont to take her away with him, all he says is, "Do you really want to go or are you just being hysterical? . . . It doesn't make any difference. I'll take you if you want to go."[63] We can't tell what Beaumont feels here, and I argue it doesn't make any difference. Hammett's interest in *The Glass Key* has been to illustrate the attempt of one man to be loyal to another in a world where such an endeavor is an anomaly.

The Glass Key is a novel of betrayal and loss. Its plot portrays a series of ironic reversals and betrayals—Bernie Despain's, Opal Madvig's of her father, Paul Madvig's of Opal, Eloise Mathews' of her husband, Taylor Henry's of Opal, Taylor Henry's betrayal of his father, Jeff Gardner's betrayal of Shad O'Rory, and climatically, Madvig's betrayal of Beaumont—all of which are shown to be connected with the all-pervading corruption of society. Crime and guilt are coextensive with society itself,[64] and betrayal comes to represent the way of life in the new society. Beaumont finds that by adhering to what is best within himself he is an outsider in this world. The novel comes the closest to being a tragic-comedy that Hammett ever wrote, and the flaws lay not within the hero but in the world outside. Unquestionably, the novel would have had greater force had Hammett more completely rendered Beaumont's inner anguish, but he lets consequences of action speak for themselves. Every character suffers by what he does or fails to do. Senator Henry must face his consequences, Madvig his, and Beaumont his. The bleakness of the moral vision is inherent in Hammett's implication that even moral action exacts a terrible price; more severe, perhaps, than immoral action. All that has been shown to have been the center of Beaumont's life is shattered—all, that is, but his adherence to truth, and it is this alone which keeps him from the decadence around him.[65] But it is a terribly lonely position to be in.

The novel ends with Ned Beaumont staring "fixedly" at a closed door, the appropriate image of a man alienated from all that has had meaning for him. It is the apt image for the alienated man who has been unconsciously victimized by his society. Despite Madvig's plea that they begin anew, Beaumont knows that it is impossible because trust is no longer a viable connection between them.

Beaumont, like Spade before him, suggests the alienated man of our times. Both discover in their search for truth that the ends of individuals and the ends of society are no longer one.

As John Paterson puts it, the detective or shamus "is the symbol of the isolated individual who, in the sense that he has been estranged from the community rather than banished from it, is an exile."[66] The superman image that comes through in Sam Spade is not found in Ned Beaumont; rather, the emphasis is on his ability to absorb terrific punishment and yet persevere in his belief in another's innocence. The will to power doesn't accomplish much: it leads to the discovery that innocence only masks another kind of betrayal. The committed individual finds his authenticity by valuation, by believing in something other than himself, but valuation is shown to be, in Beaumont, a perilous activity in the hollow society of modern America.

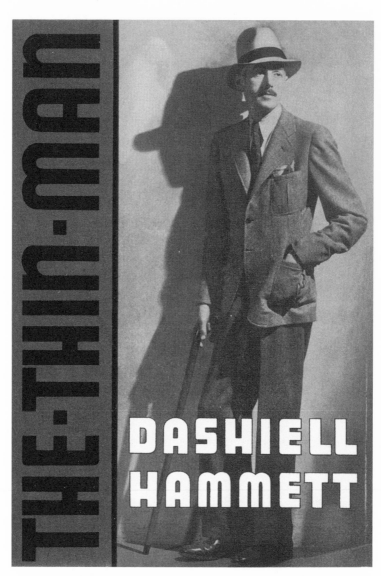

The Thin Man *was published January 8, 1934, with author Hammett's photo on the front cover. A copy of an unsigned first edition, first printing in very good plus to near fine condition in a similar condition dust jacket would be worth $7,000 to $10,000 today.*

CHAPTER SEVEN

The Thin Man:
The End Game

W HEN IT WAS PUBLISHED, Dashiell Hammett's last novel,
   The Thin Man (1934), earned glowing reviews from
ardent admirers, with Peter Quennel, in his review of the novel
in 1934, being a good example. Quennel admired several
achievements of the work:

> . . . it contains portraits, snatches of dialogue written in
> colloquial vein—and lurid glimpses of New York drink-
> ing society, that Hemingway himself could not have
> improved upon.[1]

Hammett, himself, in a 22 Jan. 1934 letter to his wife, revealed his pleasure at the book's acceptance: "First, the book is doing swell. It got very fine reviews—as you can see from the enclosed clippings—and last week sold better than any book in New York, Philadelphia, and San Francisco, besides being near the top of the list in most other cities."[2]

In the latter half of the twentieth century, however, many critics found faults with the novel, but even the most critical had to agree that it contains several good individual scenes. Few, perhaps, would go as far as Joseph T. Shaw in proclaiming that both Hammett's Nick Charles and Philip Marlowe (hero of Raymond Chandler's novels; Shaw uses *The Big Sleep* as an example of Chandler's work) are three-dimensional characters, and that in both novels character conflicts are set up, and

> The main crime and its victim are off-stage, and, while the solution of the crime is woven into the pattern of each story, it by no means constitutes the essence of the story.[3]

These lines suggest that Shaw believes *The Thin Man* to possess not only depth but resonance as well, a view that runs counter to most recent critical opinions. Presumably, from Shaw's point of view the novel is more than the sum of its parts because the action radiates meaning above and beyond the solution of the mystery.

Walter Blair argues a similar point when he says:

> Nick is very different from the Continental Op: he is attractive, sophisticated, and witty. He resembles the earlier narrator in being cynical and worldly and in being unrevealing about his emotional and intellectual

responses to most people and events. In the final novel
as in the first, the author therefore utilizes a fictional
point of view that is well adapted to the genre which he
is writing—one productive of mystery and suspense. [4]

Unfortunately Blair does not go into detail in an effort to define
that fictional point of view or to show how the action in *The
Thin Man* is handled artistically.

Another admirer of the novel is author Donald Westlake:

When I was fourteen or fifteen I read Hammett's *The
Thin Man* (the first Hammett I'd read) and it was a
defining moment. It was a sad, lonely, lost book, that
pretended to be cheerful and aware and full of good fellowship, and I hadn't known you could do that: seem to
be telling this, but really telling that; three-dimensional
writing, like three-dimensional chess. Nabokov was the
other master of that. [5]

By and large, recent critics have been rather silent on *The Thin
Man*. There are numerous short and pithy pronouncements on
the novel's worth, but almost no close analysis of its plot action
or its meaning. To my knowledge, for example, George Grella,
one of the most interesting and provocative interpreters of the
Black Mask school of writing and the hardboiled novel in general, ignores the novel almost entirely in three of his best works
on the subject. [6] David Bazelon is content to say simply that the
novel is weak because Nick Charles' "weakness is the weakness
of deliberate unconsciousness," [7] an understandable comment
from someone who believes that Hammett's art is wholly concerned with the work ethic. Ben Ray Redman sees *The Thin
Man* as an illustration of sadism and heroic drinking, [8] and
Philip Durham brushes aside serious consideration of the work

by remarking that is was obviously "written under Hollywood influence." Durham's interest is more in what *The Thin Man*, as it was originally begun, might have become. Begun in 1930, Hammett's first draft of *The Thin Man* was written in the third person, set in San Francisco, and with a "modified Op" whose main characteristic was his ghost-like, untouchable character. Hammett only completed 65 pages of this draft.[9]

Two critics who expend useful critical energy on *The Thin Man* are William Kenney and Robert I. Edenbaum. Kenney calls it a novel of parts, not a successful whole, and points to the marvelously comic scenes in the Pigiron Club, the handling of the audacious Mimi Wynant-Jorgensen, and Nora Charles' fascination with her husband's underworld connections to support his point.[10] He argues that one of the major flaws of the novel is its plot: "The plot seems too often merely a pretext for cleverly executed but unfocused individual scenes and character touches."[11] Further, Kenney believes characterization is another major problem of the novel because the murderer, Herbert Macaulay, is "the most weakly drawn character in the novel."[12] Kenney believes we are again faced with the problem we had with Owen Fitzstephan in *The Dain Curse*, Brigid O'Shaughnessy in *The Maltese Falcon*, and even Paul Madvig and Senator Henry in *The Glass Key*: the artist cannot allow us to get inside the guilty minds if mystification is to be sustained.[13] Kenney is certainly accurate in arguing that Macaulay is an unmemorable figure. Hammett managed with some skill to make Fitzstephan, O'Shaughnessy, and Henry interesting and memorable in their own right despite the limitations of his genre, but Macaulay has even less personality than a man we never meet in the novel: Clyde Wynant, the thin man of the title.

Kenney cannot find an organizing principle to *The Thin Man* and, except to say that it resembles the preceding novels in its emphasis on the loss of love between men and women and the corruption of the family, he finds little or no development of ideas or innovation in form in *The Thin Man* which might distinguish it from the earlier works.[14]

Robert Edenbaum argues that Nick Charles is the logical extension of detective Jack Rumsen of *The Glass Key*:

> That modification of the private-eye character in the direction of the cynicism and timidity of self-interest prepares the way for Hammett's last novel, *The Thin Man* . . . Nick Charles and his boozing is what happens to the Op/Spade when he gives up his role as ascetic demi-god to become husband, man of leisure, investor in futures on the stock market.[15]

In short, Edenbaum suggests the tough guy has disappeared from Hammett's pages:

> The martini-for-breakfast cracking wise of William Powell and Myrna Loy more than anything else accounts for the popularity of *The Thin Man*. Despite Nick Charles' tough manner, Hammett's tough guy has been retired for good before this book appeared.[16]

[169]

Like Kenney, Edenbaum believes *The Thin Man* lacks substantiality because it is superficial and without visionary force and, presumably, because it does not do what the preceding novels did.

But suppose Hammett has different intentions for this last novel? What bothers me about most of the negative criticisms of *The Thin Man* is that they originate from questions about what the novel is not, rather than what the novel is.

Edenbaum suggests that Hammett's power is weakened considerably by the absence of an authentic tough guy in this last novel, implying that Hammett should have kept doing what he had been doing before. I think a fairer approach would be to ask why Hammett might have chosen to alter the character of his protagonist and whether the new figure makes any significant difference in our understanding of Hammett's developing moral and social vision.

I think Hammett's new figure does make a difference, and I argue further that if we approach *The Thin Man* from this perspective we see that it is not an anomaly in Hammett's work but rather a continuation and a logical extension of the themes and concerns of the preceding novels. We noted that *The Glass Key* portrayed the destruction of Ned Beaumont's relationship with Paul Madvig and ended with him estranged from all that he had previously found meaningful. In his book *The Uncommitted*, Kenneth Keniston argues that the concept of alienation implies that "a positive relationship has ceased to exist" and that in many cases "alienation merely implies lack of any relationship at all—detachment and indifference."[17] *The Thin Man* captures this sense; without job or interest, Nick Charles is an apt post-Beaumont character. Hammett's social and moral vision has grown bleaker and bleaker as he moved from *The Dain Curse* and *The Maltese Falcon* to *The Glass Key*. This last novel, *The Thin Man*, in one sense then, is the darkest of all because it suggests the almost total alienation of modern man. If I am right, *The Thin Man* cannot then be an anomaly in Hammett's fiction.

Because the critics have been more interested in determining what the novel is not rather than what it is, they have isolated weaknesses that should more properly be seen as strengths, strengths that are intrinsically connected with Hammett's intention to render a dark vision. For example, it is accurate to call Herbert Macaulay the weakest villain Hammett ever created. Like major characters Fitzstephan and Madvig who are friends of the protagonist, Macaulay is a friend of ex-detective Nick Charles, but unlike the Op-Fitzstephen and Beaumont-Madvig relationships, the Charles-Macaulay connection is static and undeveloped. But is this necessarily a weakness in Hammett's conception? Is it not possible that Hammett intends us to notice this stasis? Similarly, should we not ask the same questions concerning the Nick and Nora relationship? It, too, seems relatively devoid of feeling and development. William Kenney comments that

> This brittle, hard-drinking, wisecracking couple seem almost as a matter of principle to avoid any direct expression of feeling for each other.[18]

Kenney apparently takes this to be a criticism of their relationship, but is it necessarily so? Can we be so very sure that a lack of direct expression of feeling is evidence that no feeling exists? Even if the answer to these questions is affirmative, does that necessarily mean the novel is flawed? I think such questions need asking, and I believe that the answers will show us that *The Thin Man* deserves a far better reputation as a work of art than has previously been conceded.

I have argued that in Hammett's earlier novels detection and human relationships have an organic connection. Spade's detection of Brigid O'Shaughnessy's guilt affects his relationship with her, and Beaumont's discovery of Paul Madvig's lack of honesty about Taylor Henry's murder affects their relationship. But in *The Thin Man*, though relationships are stated they are never allowed to develop. The discovery that Macaulay is the murderer affects neither Nick's sense of personal relationships nor his sense of himself. His detective work, unlike Spade's or Beaumont's, leads to no discovery beyond the answer to a riddle. What are we to make of this? Ought we to see this as a

[171]

weakness? I think not. Surely Hammett's point is that the quest for truth no longer carries any inherent meaning. Answers may be found, but nothing changes, and this suggests that what was once a meaningful human activity is no longer so.

Robert Edenbaum implies that Nick Charles is a tough guy *manqué* and William Kenney argues that Nick is distinguished only by a certain ironic detachment from his aimless and amoral friends."[19] Both seem to agree that Nick is a failed creation, but I do not think the character of Nick Charles is this simple. Previously, Hammett has successfully indicated the absence of values in society by locating existing values within his protagonists, but here in *The Thin Man* there is little or no emphasis on values of any kind. The famous Op/Spade/Beaumont code has all but shriveled up; Nick's articulation of a code can only be seen as a hollow echo of Hammett's former stances. In Chapter 9, for example, as Nick sees he is being forced into the Wynant case, he says:

> "I want to see the Jorgensens together at home, I want to see Macaulay, and I want to see Studsy Burke. I've been pushed around too much. I've got to see about things."

And three pages later:

> "I don't see what I'm going to do because I don't know what's being done to me. I've got to find out in my own way."[20]

Despite these declamations of determination and individualism, however, Nick continues to resist being drawn into the case, and he never again mentions his desire to know or to do anything. In fact, later in the novel he says:

"Things," I said, "riddles, lies, and I'm too old and
too tired for them to be any fun. Let's go back to San
Francisco."[21]

No comment better serves to reflect his emotional and mental
state throughout the novel. Where Hammett's earlier heroes
work to keep themselves true to their personal visions of reality
and their identity, and, like Sisyphus, continue to push their
own thing, Nick has given up. The fact that Hammett's characters become mutilated in their struggle to *become* (like Beaumont) or to preserve what they are (like Spade) is in itself a kind
of existential exaltation. But with Nick Charles the struggle has
ceased, and with its cessation, Hammett implies, the dignity
that was once man's is now no more.

A careful examination of the novel goes a long way towards
confirming such a point of view. For the first time, values are
almost nowhere apparent. In marked contrast to the earlier
works, *The Thin Man* fails to suggest the viability of any truth
or value. Hammett uses one third of his novel showing Nick
resisting Nora's interest in the Wynant affair, yet Nick's reasons
are never made clear. In *Red Harvest* the Op is pulled into the
proliferating cases by a desire to finish a job and exact personal
satisfaction, and in *The Dain Curse*, by a desire to find the
answers to what seem to be three separate cases. Spade in *The
Maltese Falcon* is drawn into the falcon affair by his desire to
help Brigid O'Shaughnessy and his continuing desire to find
the murderer of his partner. In *The Glass Key*, Ned Beaumont
enters the Henry affair initially out of loyalty to his friend Paul
Madvig, and he stays with it for the same reason. But Nick's
disinterest is repeatedly stressed. Sometimes it seems to stem
from laziness, sometimes from tiredness, and sometimes from
indifference, but Hammett consistently suggests that detective
work no longer holds value for Nick.

[173]

What conclusion can we draw from this portrayal? There surely is one. Like Beaumont, Nick is not a detective; he is only an ex-detective, now retired and living on his wife's money and stock securities. Hammett's last protagonist is no longer a member of that special species of men who choose to stand midway between criminality and the law. Rather, he chooses not to; to a great extent, he is an establishment man, with the slick manners, disinterested attitude, and the bankroll of that group. The quasi-proletarian hero—Op, Spade, Beaumont—is replaced by an ex-white collar worker whose interest in work has evaporated with his good fortune. When his wife makes repeated efforts to get him interested in Dorothy Wynant's predicament he resists:

> "Anyway, it's nothing in my life. . . . But besides I haven't the time: I'm too busy to see that you don't lose any of the money I married you for."[22]

This is partly tongue and cheek, a characteristic aspect of his ironic humor, but how much so we cannot be sure. Humor or not, Nick's point is always the same: "Let the Charleses stick to the Charleses' troubles and the Wynants stick to the Wynants'."[23] Such a statement has for the twenty-first century reader a wonderfully "relevant" sound to it: it's the uncommitted declaration which to so many of us seems partially responsible for the social failure of our time. We know that Hammett himself believed that man ought to be committed to something, not simply a hanger-on,[24] and it is hard to see how he would find Charles a positive figure.

Hammett goes out of his way to emphasize just how difficult it is to involve Nick in the action. He creates a series of episodes that function, in one way or another, to pull Nick in against his will. First there is Dorothy Wynant's plea for help, followed closely by her mother's:

"Won't you help me, Nick? We used to be friends." Her
big blue eyes were soft and appealing. . . .

"For Christ's sake, Mimi," I said, "there's a thousand detectives in New York. Hire one of them. I'm not
working at it any more."[25]

This exchange clearly reveals his uninterest.

If words won't move him, actions get a better result. The
gangster Shep Morelli comes to his apartment to proclaim
his innocence of Julia Wolf's murder and is not convinced by
Nick's argument that he is no longer a detective. The police
show up unexpectedly and Morelli panics, shooting Nick and
wounding him slightly. Nick finds himself caught up in a web
of chance and accident. Morelli had come to Nick because of
his reputation for being an on-the-level detective, and the police
had staked out the Charles' apartment because Nora's intense
interest in the Wynant-Wolf affair had led her to encourage
the Wynant-Jorgensen family to spend a lot of time at Nick and
Nora's apartment. Trapped by circumstances, Nick gives us his
"I've got to see about things" speech.[26]

Yet even now he is not committed. When a telegram is
received, supposedly from Clyde Wynant, asking Nick to
enter the case, he simply sends the telegram to the police,
paying no more attention to it. The police even request his
aid in the investigation and Nick denies he's working for
Wynant, saying: "I'm not a private detective any more. I'm
not any kind of detective," and "If people keep on pushing
me into it, I don't know how far they'll carry me."[27] He shows
no inner response to these repeated calls for help except
exasperation. His tone and oral delivery conveys, at best, his
intention to remain a passive figure, pushed along only by the
interest of others.

In some ways Hammett's exposition seems to be working tra-
ditionally—that is, the hero's importance and stature is stressed

by the fact of everyone else's need to turn to him for help. But Hammett is using this traditional form ironically. Nick Charles is more the anti-hero, resisting the call. The impotence of modern society is suggested by showing that the police need Nick's help, and Nick's lack of commitment suggests the death of the last stronghold of justice: the private eye. Hammett has commented that the society that has need of a private detective lives by questionable values,[28] but how much bleaker must it be if the need is there but there is no one who cares any longer to do the job.

If Archie Jones is correct in arguing that the private eye was created to replace the cowboy myth, to perform "the ritual cleansing of the new stables" and "to reassure the people that the lonely individual could still triumph,"[29] then Hammett's novel must, to a considerable extent, be seen as a shattering of that myth. As presented, although Nick finally ferrets out the truth, his entire behavior exudes an absence of personal commitment or satisfaction in the endeavor. He is much more the armchair detective, remote and alienated from the world he so unwillingly serves. Nick's hardboiled exterior covers only emptiness; he seems representative of the kind of figure Sheldon Grebstein describes in some of Hemingway's novels:

[176]

> This bleakness and despair, this exacerbated awareness of the betrayal of what had once been a precious innocence, and the grimly distrustful and corrosively ironic response which follow inevitably from the betrayal, compose the nucleus of the tough *Weltanschauung*.[30]

Though we are not given much information about Nick's past, a reader of Hammett's novels can sense that the betrayal which befalls Ned Beaumont in *The Glass Key* provides the Hammett perspective for Nick, his last major fictive hero. From this point of view, Nick is the only possible creation left for Hammett.

A reading such as this presupposes the kind of moral and social vision I have described. If indeed *Red Harvest* is Hammett's initial and unsuccessful search for a hero and dynamic form, and if indeed *The Dain Curse* represents Hammett's redefinition of that hero and a new direction in form, and if indeed *The Maltese Falcon* and *The Glass Key* represent Hammett's formulated vision of the dilemmas of a moral protagonist in a world devoid of values, then *The Thin Man* represents Hammett's pessimistic recognition that such men are no longer of this world. The hardboiled skin survives, but its reason for existing is gone.

Seen from this perspective, the so-called weakness of the novel in Edenbaum's and Kenney's analyses must be seen as strengths. We can now see that *The Thin Man*, though it seems considerably different in style and form from its predecessors, has its place in the total spectrum of Hammett's work. It is the novel of the end: it evacuates from the hardboiled hero precisely those qualities the other four novels tried so subtly to render. The relationship between Nick and Macaulay is devoid of meaning because both are indifferent or incapable of dynamic relationships. The heroic code is dissipated in Nick because he has nothing within him to make it a meaningful stimulus for action. The earlier heroes had direction and purpose, or found it, but Nick has nothing to hold on to except perhaps Nora, Nora's money, and his wry disinterest in the world around him. The static world of the novel is best described by Nick himself at the very end. In response to Nora's question concerning what the end result will be of all that has taken place, he answers:

> "Nothing new. They'll go on being Mimi and Dorothy and Gilbert just as you and I will go on being us and the Quinns will go on being the Quinns. Murder doesn't

round out anybody's life except the murdered's and sometimes the murderer's."[31]

For the first time in Hammett's work, detection fails to become a metaphor for life. Not only is there no education in moral terms, there is no change at all. Previously, detective work had, like a pebble dropped into a stagnant pool, created ripples of significance and meaning. In *The Thin Man* the pebble is dropped—the truth is discovered—but the stagnant waters are too turgid to respond. The earlier novels suggest that very few, perhaps only the detective, learned from experience. This novel makes it clear that no one learns, no one grows, no one profits in any meaningful way.

In short, the purported weaknesses of the novel—the lack of characterization, the superficiality of the hero, and the lack of resonance—become emblems of Hammett's dark vision of America's loss of a hero. *The Thin Man* illustrates the loss of self in modern times perhaps more completely than any other detective novel in the 1920s–1930s. Perhaps it is this recognition which prompts Ross Macdonald to say:

"Hammett was the first American writer to use the detective-story for the purposes of a major novelist, to present a vision, blazing if disenchanted, of our lives."[32]

Hammett creates a protagonist who lacks even the impulse to dream of a better world. Though Nick is convinced of the unreality of the world around him, he feels no pain as a result of this perception. It may be that we are to interpret his obsessive drinking and hedonistic urges as a sign of his inner need to numb his sensibilities, but we cannot be sure. It may be that it would be more fitting to read his indulgences in drink and wit as the Hammett hero's last attempt to keep his distance from the corruption surrounding him.

The other characters in the novel express a negation of
life through their actions, but Nick and Nora seem somehow
different. Judged from conventional standards, their relationship seems superficial, but in the context of the novel their
relationship seems the best possible. In a world where everyone
else takes themselves so terribly seriously, often at the expense
of others, Nick and Nora's ability to laugh at each other and
themselves seems healthy and refreshing. Their inability to
communicate on a direct emotional level shows them to be
creatures of Hammett's dark new world, but they seem free of
the worst of that world. Their relationship seems to have its own
rules and game theory; less a traditional marriage and more
an understanding, they remind a reader of Lillian Hellman's
description of her relationship with Hammett:

> We never again spoke of that night because, I think, he
> was ashamed of the angry gesture that made him once
> again the winner in the game that men and women play
> against each other, and I was ashamed that I caused
> myself to lose so often.[33]

Hammett and Hellman fought hard, drank hard, and laughed
hard together, and Nick and Nora do the same. In comparison
with the other marriages in the novel, Nick and Nora have
something going for them. They understand one another and
they interact. Where the other couples have surely lost connection, Nick and Nora seem right for one another in regard to
their tastes and level of wit.

[179]

In fact, much of *The Thin Man* evinces a serious authorial concern for the way people relate. Hammett narrows and
compresses his social vision markedly. His focus is on the
disintegration of the family unit.[34]

The usual Hammett theme of deception is almost entirely
illustrated through the portrayals of the various families in the

novel. Such compression of focus suggests Hammett's overriding concern with the most corrosive of forces in modern America: family breakdown. Edenbaum remarks that

> *The Thin Man* is perhaps less concerned with murder and the private-eye than with the people around the murder—with a wide range of social types spiritually sibling to the Alfred G. Packer of the long entry Gilbert Wynant reads in *Celebrated Criminal Cases of America.* The man-eaters Mimi, Dorothy, and Gilbert Wynant; Christian Jorgensen, Herbert Macaulay, the Quinns, the Edges; as well as underworld characters like Shep Morelli and Julia Wolf are little less cannibalistic than Packer. . .[35]

Edenbaum is quite right. *The Thin Man* is the least hero-centered novel of the group. It is most like *Red Harvest* in its social emphasis. Everyone in the novel exerts a negative influence on a family, and Hammett's intention is to explore and expose the hollowness of modern society.

Packer, with his five companions in the wilds of the Colorado mountains, are joined together by their common desire for gold. As Packer tells the story, when the group finds starvation imminent, it agrees to a survival compact, a family agreement to eat the fleshiest members first. When only Packer and a man named Bell are left, they enter "into a solemn compact that as we were the only ones left we would stand by each other whatever befell, rather than harm each other we would die of starvation."[36] As Packer tells it, Bell breaks the compact and tries to kill him, thus forcing him to kill Bell first and to use him for food. Of course, this family compact turns out to be a fabrication. Under the pretense of human concern, Packer attempted to save his own neck. The truth is, he killed all five, obviously in hopes of keeping all the expected treasure for himself, and ate their flesh to sustain himself.

Edenbaum is right to argue that man's cannibalism is the major theme in *The Thin Man*. The "true" Packer case reflects on the fiction just as the fiction reflects on life in modern America as Hammett sees it. The theme of the Packer story is similar to that of William Golding's *Lord of the Flies* or Robert Ardrey's *African Genesis*: in a state of isolation, man will revert back to his innate primitive nature.

The Packer story reflects in a variety of ways the main action of the novel. The "truth" as Packer tells it turns out to be a tissue of lies just as the "truth" as articulated by Mimi, Dorothy, Gilbert, and Macaulay turns out to be webs of deception. Further, the Packer story functions as a paradigm of all the family relationships pictured in the novel. What we see in the Wynant-Jorgensen family, the Quinn family, the Edge family, and the Nunheim family is cannibalism masquerading behind the illusion of the family compact. In each case, the motivation for their vicious behavior is a combination of greed and a feeling of the necessity of self-survival, precisely the ingredients of the Packer story.

The novel opens, in fact, with Dorothy Wynant's description of her broken family and her hatred for her mother, her father, and her brother.[37] As the novel develops, we see the mutual hatred, distrust, and greed which motivates the Wynant-Jorgensen family. Dorothy is repeatedly beaten by Mimi[38] and Hammett's diction suggests the viciousness underlying the act: "Mimi slashed Dorothy across the mouth with the back of her hand."[39] Dorothy tells us that her stepfather Christian Jorgensen intends to stay married to Mimi only so long as her money holds out[40] and that he married her only for her alimony-rich bank account.[41] Jorgensen, it turns out, not only violates the marriage compact by committing adultery with Olga Fenton[42] but has violated if from the beginning by marrying for the wrong reason—revenge rather than love—and being a bigamist.

Jorgensen's ruthless approach to marriage is mirrored by Mimi's behavior. Discovering that Jorgensen is really her former husband Clyde's rival Victor Rosewater,[43] and suspecting that Jorgensen-Rosewater married her solely for revenge, Mimi is more than willing to frame him for Julia Wolf's murder:

> "That son of a bitch made a fool of me, Nick, an out and out fool, and now he's in trouble and expects me to help him. I'll help him." She put a hand on my knee and her pointed nails dug into my flesh. "The police, they don't believe me. How can I make them believe that he's lying, that I know nothing more than I've told them about the murder?"[44]

Initially out of revenge against Clyde and for monetary gain, and now out of spite for having been played a fool by Jorgensen, Mimi is willing to send her husband Jorgensen to the gas chamber by holding back evidence that would implicate Clyde. She follows her most primitive instincts, wanting to strike back at the man who has hurt her. All pretense of a civilized relationship is dropped.

Affection is never given freely in the Wynant-Jorgensen family. When Gilbert feels that Dorothy's attraction to Nick threatens Gilbert's position as Dorothy's knight, he tries to gain respect in Dorothy's eyes by purposely lying to her that he has seen their father and knows who killed Julia. He lies out of hate and jealousy of Nick:

> "I was—it was— I suppose it was jealousy really." He looked up at me now and his face was pink. "You see,

Dorry used to look up to me and think I knew more than anybody else about everything and—you know—she'd come to me if there was anything she wanted to know and she always did what I told her, and then, when she got to seeing you, it was different. She looked up to you and respected you more— She naturally would, I mean, she'd've been silly if she hadn't, because there's no comparison, of course . . ."[45]

As Nick himself describes the Wynant-Jorgensens:

"There doesn't seem to be a single one of them in the family—now that Mimi's turned against her Chris— who has even the slightest reasonably friendly feeling for any of the others, and yet there's something very alike in all of them."[46]

The similarity is their equal lack of human feeling for any one other than themselves, Hammett suggests that intense self-interest only reveals the hollowness that lies within. Gilbert is only able to measure his identity by an external pecking order; his actions reveal his recognition that there exists no sound basis for a relationship between himself and his sister. He confuses affection with worship. Mimi's sole desire is to sell herself to the highest bidder, and toward the end of the novel Hammett illustrates the absurdity of this motive for living when he shows her unwittingly cheating herself by agreeing to Macaulay's proposal.

The other families in this novel are likewise shattered by distrust and greed. Harrison Quinn, we are told, lusts after Dorothy Wynant and hopes to divorce his wife and marry her. Alice Quinn, his wife, remembers when "he had muscles," probably her equivalent of manhood, and later admits to Nick and Nora that she stays with him only "for his money."[47] The last we hear of their relationship is that Harrison has disappeared from home.

The Alice-Harrison Quinn marriage is mirrored by the Art Nunheim-Miriam relationship. Nunheim, too, is unfaithful to his lover, and neither has any respect for the other. As she puts it,

> "I don't like crooks, and even if I did, I wouldn't like crooks that are stool-pigeons, and if I liked crooks that are stool-pigeons, I still wouldn't like you."[48]

She walks out on Nunheim, and he is killed trying to shake Macaulay down for additional money.

Lastly, of course, we are told very early that Clyde Wynant's adultery with Julia Wolf was what caused the breakup between Mimi and him. William Kenney sums up his view of personal relationships in the novel by saying:

> Moreover, as if to right some strange balance, Hammett depicts in this novel a series of relationships in which the strongest emotion either partner seems capable of feeling for the other is contempt.[49]

[184]

I would add that the feeling of contempt is joined by the feeling of hate and the desire to survive financially. Though the novel deals explicitly only with the murders of three people—Julia Wolf, Clyde Wynant, and Art Nunheim—it implicitly pictures a society of cannibals.

One possible implication of Hammett's preoccupation with broken and alienated families is that, however incompletely or obliquely he articulates it, he perceived and gave warning to a birth of an attitude that Kenneth Keniston defines as part of a larger alienated pattern:

> Central to alienation is a deep and pervasive mistrust
> of any and all commitments, be they to other people, to
> groups, to American culture, or even to the self. Most
> basic here is the distrust of other people in general—a
> low and pessimistic view of human nature.[50]

Though *The Thin Man* is set in New York City, and written by
Hammett while living in New York, the insecurity, violence, and
the failure to communicate on any level but the most primitive
suggest his recognition that the Hollywood dream has become
the American nightmare.[51] Philip Durham refers to *The Thin
Man* as being "obviously written under Hollywood influence,"
by which he meant to imply that it was superficial.[52] But I think
his comment carries more weight than he realized. The Packer
story is an exemplar of an aspect of America's historical move
westward in pursuit of the golden dream of success. The uncon-
scionable rapacity of Packer mirrors what befalls the human
race when it reaches the land of golden illusions. By letting the
action speak for itself, Hammett raises the grim spector of what
modern society has become.

Hammett reinforces his conception of a hollow world by
emphasizing the problematic nature of identities in the novel.
He presents us with a series of characters whose names turn out
to be false. In *The Maltese Falcon* we noted that he employed
deceptive images and details to illustrate that a character's outward appearance in no way reflected his true reality.[53] This same
disjunction between one's appearance and one's real nature is
embodied in *The Thin Man* by the uncertainty of one's name.
Jorgensen is discovered to be Victor Rosewater; Julia Wolf is
Rhoda Stewart, finally Nancy Kane; Albert Norman turns out
to be Arthur Nunheim; and Sparrow is discovered to be Jim
Brophy. Nick Charles' real family name is Charalambides.[54]
The living Clyde Wynant turns out to have been dead from

the beginning. Almost all of the action in the novel emanates from the assumption that Wynant is alive, an assumption that proves as misleading and hollow of truth as everything else. Even when his body is discovered, his identity is still obscured by the false signs of baggy clothes and a belt buckle carrying the initials D.W.Q.

Undoubtedly, the greatest triumph of *The Thin Man* is its plot. For the first time, Hammett makes plot primary, and characterization secondary. As a mystery-detective plot it is a *tour de force*. The entire structure is built around the idea that the suspected murderer will be dead from the beginning, himself a victim of murder. The ingenuity of such an idea is well proven by its finding repeated use by later writers. Raymond Chandler employs this device in his first novel, *The Big Sleep* (1939), and Ross Macdonald repeats it with variations in *The Wycherly Woman* (1961) and *The Underground Man* (1971).

One point in using such a structure is to suggest the problematic nature of reality, a theme all of Hammett's novels stress. The reader is consistently misled by red herrings, although Hammett plants enough clues that he cannot be accused of violating the fair-play doctrine. We are told early, for example, that Clyde Wynant gave Macaulay power of attorney over his estate and though this turns out to be untrue, Macaulay supposedly does possess that power. Later we are told that Macaulay had once lost a large amount of money on the stock market and therefore can infer he has need of money.[55] Therefore he has a motive for murder. The main clue, or course, is the fact that no one sees Wynant though the first three-fourths of the novel; all we have are letters and telegrams supposedly from him. The triumph of the plot as a mystery plot is that these clues go almost unnoticed because everything else points to Wynant as the murderer of Julia Wolf. Only Nick's skepticism seems to point to other possibilities. When the truth is uncovered, we can see its probabilities, but throughout the novel we are taken in by Macaulay's rendition of reality. He literally creates his own mystery fiction, planting clues (red herrings) and suggesting a host of possible alternatives for the police to examine.

Hammett is far more skillful in plotting *The Thin Man* than critics have realized. Aside from the ingenuity of its basic conception, the plot is shown to be an accurate reflection of Hammett's conception of mankind. It illustrates and gives resonance to Hammett's themes of greed and savagery.

If, for example, we examine Macaulay's actions in the plot we note that all are precipitated by his greed and his instinct for self-survival. His murder of Julia Wolf is necessitated by his discovery that she has a lover—Face Peppler—who is about to be freed from jail. Knowing that she has always been frightened and uneasy over his murder of Wynant, Macaulay surmises that once Wolf has a chance she will run away with Peppler, and perhaps reveal his crime. He therefore kills her to prevent discovery. Greed and financial self-survival drove him to murder Clyde Wynant, and here greed and self-survival drive him to kill her. Macaulay had to kill Wynant who had discovered that Macaulay had been cheating him. Wynant's savage murder recalls Packer:

[187]

> "He'd been sawed up in pieces and buried in lime
> or something so there wasn't much flesh left on him,
> according to the report I got. . ."[56]

As Nick puts it, two of the murders were "obviously done in cold blood."[57] Macaulay's murder of Nunheim was another motivated by greed and the instinct for self-survival.

But the plot does more than simply unmask a villain because it shows that the villain survives only because of corresponding greed in those around him. In the last fourth of the novel, Hammett reverses our growing expectation that Macaulay may have been lying all along by bringing forward two characters who claim they, too, have seen Wynant: Gilbert and his mother, Mimi. Gilbert lies to rise in his sister's eyes, as aforementioned, and his selfishness and meanness of spirit temporarily aid Macaulay, first by directing attention away from himself, and secondly by giving him the idea to use Mimi's own greed and selfishness to cheat her out of most of her fortune. Hammett's point seems to be that Macaulay almost gets away with everything because everyone else is corrupt as well. The implication we draw is that cannibals like Macaulay can feast off of others because the world is so devoid of values that he can appear as a natural part of the landscape.

A plot such as this emphasizes the interdependence of the criminal and his society and suggests that a Macaulay is only an exaggerated form of a general malaise. By portraying society as an unwitting accomplice to Macaulay, Hammett suggests that modern man is alienated and empty because society itself has lost its soul. George Grella has commented that Hammett's works imply, but do not articulate fully, "an urban chaos, devoid of spiritual and moral values, pervaded by viciousness and random savagery."[58] Seen this way, crime is not a temporary

aberration but a ubiquitous fact.

Wylie Sypher in speaking of the nineteenth century and the modern existentialists says that one question which these novelists pose is, "What does experience mean after the self has been diminished, or perhaps, has vanished?"[59] Though Hammett cannot rightly be called an existentialist, *The Thin Man* and even *The Glass Key* can certainly be seen as a step in that direction. Hammett's rendering of Nick Charles, as well as the others in the novel, suggest that what he sees in the modern world around him is the loss of the authentic self. If, as Sypher argues, the existential question is "honesty," a searching for the authentic self,[60] can we not say that Hammett too has been concerned with this impulse in his creations Sam Spade and Ned Beaumont, and that Nick Charles *et al.* embody the loss of this impulse? The comic tone of the novel masks the tragic vision lying beneath and lends to the events a sense of the absurd.

The Thin Man is Hammett's bleakest novel because it posits an entropic vision of man. The moral energy of his earlier heroes becomes squandered in the aimless motions of Nick Charles. The movement from the rough and brutally instinctive Op in *Red Harvest* to the cool and sophisticated Nick Charles is a drift towards inertia and *ennui*. Similar to Meursault in Camus' *The Stranger*, Nick is willing to surrender to a kind of comic neutrality, a distrust in actions that just six years ago had been his existence.[61] His will to act has been dissipated, and even when his analytic mind is forced into action and he discovers the truth, nothing changes. All will remain as it was. Hammett's heroes have been measured by what they *did*; identity was a matter of *doing*, a doctrine quite amenable to the existentialist. André Malraux, André Gide, and Albert Camus were all admirers of Hammett.[62] Gide praised Hammett's rendering of deception in *Red Harvest* because he thought it was so truthful to experience.[63] What would probably be as satisfying to such writers is Hammett's portrayal of man's second fall, to use Martin Heidegger's words, the fall from authenticity.[64]

Finally, even detective work in the novel is conceived as a matter of appearance, not truth. Nick's description of the way real detectives work defines the authenticity of guilt or innocence as largely a matter of probabilities:

> "You find the guy you think did the murder and you slam him in the can and let everybody know you think he's guilty and put his picture all over newspapers, and the District Attorney builds up the best theory he can

on what information you've got and meanwhile you pick up additional details here and there, and people who recognize his picture in the paper—as well as people who'd think he was innocent if you hadn't arrested him—come in and tell you things about him and presently you've got him sitting in the electric chair."[65]

This construct-a-villain approach works in this novel—Macaulay is guilty—but the implication of such a doctrine is disturbing. Justice becomes a matter of good advertising and considerable luck; were police forces manned by people as intuitively bright as Nick turns out to be—he reconstructs the *gestalt* of the crime perfectly—then perhaps such an approach would be efficacious, but the novel makes it clear that the truth-conscious private eye is all but gone, and that leaves at best, a Guild, and at worst, a brutal and stupid Andy.

The moral vision of *The Thin Man* is dark indeed. In it we sense most acutely the emptiness which underlies human existence. At his best, Nick Charles is a residue of Hammett's earlier figures, hardboiled people who would sacrifice all for a piece of the truth. They, at least, had the inner strength to will their own worlds into being, even if it meant making them totally alien to the world around them. In its presentation of the loss of will and belief in truth and justice, *The Thin Man* is Hammett's rendition of the end game.

CHAPTER EIGHT

Conclusion:
Form and Substance:
An Overview

A CONSIDERATION OF THE DEVELOPING moral and social vision of the five novels aids greatly in any attempt to determine Hammett's contribution to the detective forma and to evaluate his success as an artist.

[191]

The traditional detective story is comic in form, and in all, whether by Edgar Allan Poe, Arthur Conan Doyle, Dorothy Sayers, Ellery Queen, Sue Grafton, or Tony Hillerman, one can locate at least four relatively consistent patterns.

1. First, the endings always portray an expiation of evil in the existing society;

A QUARTERLY JOURNEL DEVOTED TO THE APPRECIATION
OF
MYSTERY, DETECTIVE AND SUSPENSE FICTION
Volume 8   Number 2
February 1975

The original versions of this concluding chapter and of this
book's bibliography originally appeared in the February 1975
issue of The Armchair Detective, *volume 8: number 2.*

2. Secondly, there is always an emphasis on order, an order
   that comes about through the unraveling of the mystery;
3. Third, to one degree or another the detective's skill in
   handling his world is stressed and glorified; and
4. Lastly, the traditional novel usually concludes with a sense
   of the renewal of society, generally marked by a return to
   the everyday rhythms of life pictured—or implied—before
   the commission of the crime.

What is particularly interesting about Hammett is that he
uses essentially these same patterns but with a difference: he
complicates, modulates, and expands them to carry his peculiar
thematic thrust. Raymond Chandler has argued that the *Black
Mask* story put its emphasis on individual scenes rather than
the denouement at the end:

> "...a good plot was one which made good scenes. The
> ideal mystery was one you would read if the end was
> missing."[1]

In the traditional detective story everything works toward the
revelation at the end, but in the hardboiled tradition each scene
ideally contains "Its own denouement of revelation or action."[2]
Hammett discovered this technique and used it to give depth
and resonance to his vision.

When we open a traditional detective novel, we know pretty
much what to expect from its form. We know a crime will be
committed, and we know that the detective will solve it by the
end. Our pleasure comes, at least in part, by participating in the
mystification with the hero and trying, with him, to discover
the correct connections. Part of the aesthetic pleasure comes
at the end when, though we have failed to keep pace with the
hero's reasoning powers, we see how we have been misled, and

yet told all, by the artist. The triumph lies in the clear concealment of clues. Like a good riddle, the writer conceals only to disclose when ready, and the catharsis is one of satisfaction. It is an all's-well-that-ends-well form. In this sense, the form of the traditional detective story is comic, and, as W. H. Auden suggests in "The Guilty Vicarage," it even has dimly glimpsed metaphysical implications of a divine comedy, a journey toward a revelation and judgment.[3]

Hammett, however, modifies this comic form towards a more complicated ironic one, one more suited to his ambiguous and problematic moral vision. We can return to the analogs with Renaissance drama that we have noted earlier and suggest that the difference between Hammett comedy and traditional detective comedy is the difference between Jonsonian comedy and Shakespearean, or even Shakespeare's problem comedies and his earlier romantic comedies. Jonson's Jacobean comedy darkened and dimmed with irony the earlier Elizabethan comic light in much the same way as Hammett's darkened the traditional detective story. The bringing together of the ironic and comic give Hammett's novels a resonance and power not previously felt in the detective genre. A final review of the five novels may help to clarify Hammett's contribution to the detective form and to suggest the full range of his moral vision.

The most allegorical of the five, in some ways the most expansive in its image of pervasive evil, *Red Harvest* is, nevertheless, ironic comedy. The world of disorder becomes a world of order and evil is expunged; yet Hammett leaves us with the sense that such renovation is at best temporary. It is an ironic ending. The delicate balance is suggested by Hammett's indication that Personville is under martial law at the end, and people being what they are in the novel, it is hard to imagine that his sweet-smelling rose will not soon wither. The usual comic emphasis on renewal is here severely limited and qualified.

The sense of order we normally feel in the discovery scene of a detective novel is altered as well. Hammett moves his emphasis from the who or what question to the how: how to do a job. The Op's victory at the end comes through his discovery of how to operate in the Poisonville world. There is satisfaction in watching the Op orchestrate the destruction of the villains in such a way that they defeat themselves. His sense of his own vulnerability makes more satisfying our sense that he plays the game as well as it could have been played given the conditions of Poisonville. By such portrayal, Hammett seriously qualifies the comic thrust. Throughout, we have not been allowed merely to assume victory for the Op; we have been made to experience the ambiguous and problematic nature of the game itself. The plot is finally less important than the scenes, the end less crucial than the process.

The Dain Curse, on the other hand, more closely imitates the traditional comic form. Owen Fitzstephan, the evil force in the novel, is exposed and rendered harmless to society by the end, and though Aaronia Haldron is never tried in court and Mrs. Fink is never found, the immediately corrupting forces in the novel are discharged from the present society. Similar to the traditional detective novel, the mystery of *The Dain Curse* is a causal question—who or what lies behind the curse?—and the detective comes to perceive the only possible answer, the gestalt of the disparate elements, and the reader's confusion and mystification is removed and replaced by clarity.

But we do not feel satisfied. The peculiar success of *The Dain Curse* can be explained, I think, by Hammett's failure to harmonize his form with his substance. Hammett chooses to employ the traditional comic detective form, a form in which the denouement overshadows the parts, and yet we realize by the end that his substantive interest has been in the developing struggle between the Op and Owen Fitzstephan. We recognize that the Op's skill lies not so much in acting as in perceiving, seeing into the nature of the world around him, and the epistemological emphasis throughout suggests that the novel is partly about the problem of perception. The central contrast is between Fitzstephan and the Op, a contrast between romantic delusions and skeptical realism. Because Hammett has chosen the traditional detective form, one that emphasizes obfuscation and deemphasizes the individual scene, this character conflict is not developed as clearly as it could be.

The result is that in *The Dain Curse* Hammett fails to write either a good traditional detective story or a good problem comedy. The comic elements are all present—Fitzstephan is punished appropriately by his own stratagems, Gabrielle Leggett flowers in the hands of the Collinsons, the Collinson family regains fullness by the adoption of Gabrielle, and the forces of evil are either killed, imprisoned, or scattered—and yet Hammett is not able to harmonize his preparation scenes with the discovery scene at the end. The usual Hammett stress on the ambiguity of life and the savagery of man's nature, on the other hand, is also incomplete because, having decided to make the discovery scene prominent, he cannot develop in depth the individual scenes. The need to mystify prohibits emphasis on the process of detection, and therefore the moral and ethical dilemmas of the Op and His struggle with Fitzstephan are not able to find adequate expression.

The Maltese Falcon, however, successfully weds form and vision. The ending of the novel creates the delicate balance which is particularly the Hammett mark. There is expiation of particular evil, yet the suggestion of little or no improvement of existing society. Brigid is jailed, Gutman killed, and the others imprisoned, but the world goes on as before. The stupidity of the police and the inflexibility of the district attorney remain, and there is no evidence that the characteristics of greed, viciousness, and falseness which the villains have represented here in any way disappeared or have been attenuated in the larger society.

The ending of the novel is formally perfect. The three mysteries—who killed Archer, what is to be the relationship between Spade and Brigid, and where and what is the Maltese Falcon—are all resolved in the final scenes. Order replaces dissonance and disorder when these mysteries are unraveled. Spade's rejection of Brigid produces the greatest satisfaction because it harmonizes with, and is precipitated by, his clear-eyed view of the nature of reality. The threatening possibility that he may fall to Brigid's temptations is shown to be an illusion, and though we do not laugh when he turns her in, there is a comic rightness to it all: she gets what she deserves and least expects.

The Maltese Falcon puts the emphasis on the hero as actor. Like Jonson's Volpone, Spade knows the nature of his world, and knows that to be effective he must appear to be of that world in all respects. His success lies in his ability to outwit the knaves at their own game. Unlike Volpone, Spade does not make the comic error at the end; he does not lose perspective and become a fool. He does not let his own roguery and his knowledge of roguery, his ability to play the rogue's game, corrupt his own detachment. In this way the question often raised of his moral superiority is placed properly—it is not the real question. Gutman and the others think of themselves as rogues, but end as fools, and because of this, their fate suggests that folly is in the egotism of roguery. This comic resolution produces a sense of poetic justice, and we laugh at their failure.

But though Spade is victorious, renewal is nowhere apparent in the society. Spade ends an outsider, shut off from his loyal secretary by her failure to understand the meaning of his rejection of Brigid. Perhaps the potential of man and society is imaged in

[197]

of the mystery, yet even this release is modified by our recognition that such skill no longer brings meaning to the possessor. There is victory without measurable result. The ending suggests no renewal; all will go on as before.

The game is all that is left in *The Thin Man*. Nick and Nora represent the kind of wit and flexibility that means survival in a lost world. The novel is genuinely funny, and despite its darker overtones, we find pleasure in observing two people who have learned to live with some style and grace in an otherwise witless and graceless world.

Surely, then, one of the most interesting things about Hammett is his attempt to use the comic form to render a serious moral and social vision. Throughout his major novels, he strrives to adjust the detective form to suit his thematic interests, and what results is a kind of problem comedy. He expands the range of the comic form by making it unsettle us rather than relieve us. With the exception of *The Dain Curse*, the plotting of the novels is extremely well handled. In each, the plot strands point to larger, more informing issues, issues concerning the nature of American society, the viability of the moral and ethical hero in a fallen world, the problematic nature of reality, and the problem of identity. Detection as a process is revivified as Hammett examines the dilemmas of pragmatic, morally self-conscious heroes who attempt to do their job efficiently while holding on to their own authenticity.

[200]

As we move from *Red Harvest* to *The Dain Curse* to *The Maltese Falcon* to *The Glass Key* and finally to *The Thin Man* we increasingly become aware of a darkening authorial vision. *Red Harvest*, with its allegorical typology, represents in full the Hammett world, complete in its portrayal of the infectious mole within human nature. As we have seen, one of the problems Hammett articulates in this first novel is how inescapably ironic must be the ethical man's position in a corrupt world, and it is the problem he repeatedly examines from varying perspectives hereafter. With the creation of Sam Spade, Hammett finds a viable hero, one who is finally able to harmonize his external existence with his internal self, but the Hammett irony persists: to affirm one's authenticity is to necessarily be unlike everyone else.

The Glass Key develops the theme of alienation by focusing on society's devastating influence on the committed man. Beaumont's search for the truth leads ironically to betrayal and to the discovery that, despite good faith and almost superhuman endeavor, human relationships are at best illusory. The total estrangement of the Hammett hero from this society is painfully rendered in *The Glass Key*, and in his final novel, *The Thin Man*, Hammett extends to its typical conclusion this pattern of the mutilated American hero. The loss of inner integrity and commitment embodied in the ex-detective Nick Charles reflects Hammett's pessimistic conclusion that *doing* and *being* are forever disjoined, forever separated from dynamic and meaningful connection. In the earlier novels, the hardboiled cover had a *raison d'etre*; its necessity reflected not only the viciousness of the outside world but as well a commitment by the protagonist to protect what lay within his inner being. But in Nick Charles the hardboiled attitude is only a stance, devoid of meaningful connection with the internal self. Living off the society he distrusts and views with contempt, Nick Charles is content to please himself. Hedonism replaces valuation, and the Hammett vision closes on that note.

[201]

To see the novels as I have argued points, I think, to at least one reason Hammett never again wrote a major novel after *The Thin Man*; he had no more to say. He had worked out as far as he could the possibilities of the questions he had raised concerning individual man and society.

Like Nick Charles, he may have succumbed to ennui. There is an order, a beginning, middle, and end to the moral vision he creates as he moves from *Red Harvest* to *The Thin Man*, but his inability to change direction or to revivify his perceptions mark him as a minor writer. We must, however, acknowledge that what he did was done almost perfectly. *The Maltese Falcon* and *The Thin Man* are triumphs in form and substance, and their influence is strongly felt in the best writers of the genre today. He continues to be read, and he continues to be something more than another detective story writer for those who feel he is a serious writer—serious in form and in substance.

Notes

All citations from Dashiell Hammett's novels refer to the Library of America collected edition *Complete Novels* published in New York in 1999.

Preface: If You Haven't Read Thompson

1. Julian Symons, *Dashiell Hammett* (San Diego: Harcourt Brace Jovanovich, 1985), p. 71.

2. *The Critical Response to Dashiell Hammett*, ed. Christopher Metress (Westport, CT/London: Greenwood, 1994), p. xxv.

Introduction: In Hammett Country

1. To meet reader demand, the book was reprinted twice (in 1978 and 1980) in trade paperback by the original publisher.

2. In my just-completed definitive biography of Hammett (*A Man Called Dash*), there are over 950 chapter notes.

Chapter Two: Moral Vision: What and Why

1. "The Literature of the Thriller: A Critical Study," *Diss.* Kansas 1967, pp. 60–61.

2. "The Gangster Novel: The Urban Pastoral," *Tough Guy Writers of the Thirties*, ed. David Madden (Carbondale: Southern Illinois Press, 1968), p. 197.

3. "The Poetics of the Private-Eye: The Novels of Dashiell Hammett," *Tough Guy Writers*, pp. 102–103; reprinted in Metress, p. 178.

4. Sheldon Grabstein, "The Tough Hemingway and His Hardboiled Children," *Tough Guy Writers*, p. 22.

5. *Love and Death in the American Novel* (New York: Criterion Books, Inc., 1960), p. 476.

6. "An Imaginary Interview," tr. Malcolm Cowley, *New Republic*, CX (February 7, 1944), p. 186.

7. "Metamorphoses of Leatherstocking," *Literature in America*, ed. Philip Roth (New York: Meridian Books, 1957), p. 442.

8. Letter to Mrs. Blanche Knopf, March 20, 1928, from *Selected Letters of Dashiell Hammett 1921–1960*, ed. Richard Layman with Julie M. Rivett (Washington, D.C.: Counterpoint, 2001), p. 47.

9. Hammett, "The Need for Tempo in the Contemporary Novel," *Fighting Words*, ed. Donald Ogden Stewart (New York: Harcourt, Brace, and Company, 1940), pp. 56–57. The use of italics for emphases are Hammett's.

10. Boucher quoted in William F. Nolan, *Dashiell Hammett: A Casebook* (Santa Barbara: McNally and Loftin, 1969), p. 5.

11. "The Simple Art of Murder," *The Art of the Mystery Story*, ed. Howard Haycraft (New York: Simon and Schuster, 1946), pp. 234–5.

Chapter Three: *Red Harvest*: The Pragmatic and Moral Dilemma

1. Quoted in Nolan, p. 46.

2. Ibid., pp. 48–9.

3. *Blood Money*, though written first (1927), is a combination of two novelettes, "The Big Knockover" and "$106,000 Blood Money," which first appeared in *Black Mask* February and May, 1927. Though I am not going to discuss it here, its themes are similar to the other five novels, especially in its presentation of an ambiguous hero.

4. "The Literature of the Thriller: A Critical Study," *Diss.* Kansas 1967, p. 54.

5. "The Poetics of the Private-Eye: The Novels of Dashiell Hammett," *Tough Guy Writers*, p. 91.

6. "The Dashiell Hammett Tradition and the Modern Detective Novel," *Diss.* Michigan 1964, p. 94.

7. Ibid., p. 95.

8. Dashiell Hammett, *Red Harvest*, p. 5.

9. Ibid., p. 9.

10. Ibid., p. 10.

11. Ibid.

12. Nolan, p. 47.

13. *Red Harvest*, p. 38.

14. Ibid., pp. 39-40.

15. "A Note of Imitation and Theme," *Journal of Aesthetics and Art Criticism*, XIII (1954–5), p. 268.

16. *Red Harvest*, pp. 54.

17. Ibid., p. 53.

18. Ibid., p. 55.

19. *The Moral Vision of Jacobean Tragedy* (Madison: The University of Wisconsin Press, 1960), p. 108.

20. *Red Harvest*, p. 55.

21. Ibid., p. 56.

22. Ibid., p. 57.

23. Ibid.

24. Ibid., p. 60.

25. Latin for "law of retribution."

26. *Red Harvest*, p. 38.

27. William Shakespeare, *The Tragedy of Hamlet*, ed. G. R. Hibbard, V. ii, lines 10–11, (Oxford, New York: Oxford University Press, 1987), p. 335.

28. *Red Harvest*, p. 65.

29. Ibid., p. 70.

30. Ibid., p. 72.

31. Ibid., p. 75.

32. Ibid., p. 103.

33. Ibid., p. 72.

34. Ibid., p. 164.

35. Ibid., p. 178.

36. Ibid., p. 102.

37. Ibid., pp. 103–104.

38. Ibid., p. 104. My italics for emphasis.

39. "The Poetics of the Private-Eye: The Novels of Dashiell Hammett," *Tough Guy Writers*, p. 82.

40. *Red Harvest*, p. 101.

41. Ibid., p. 126.

42. Ibid., p. 127.

43. Ibid., p. 129.

44. Ibid.

45. Ibid., p. 135.

46. Ibid., p. 136.

47. Ibid., p. 137.

48. Ibid. The italics are mine for emphasis.

49. *The Uncommitted: Alienated Youth in American Society* (New York: Dell Publishing, 1970), pp. 400–403. Keniston presents a very useful division and analysis of various kinds of alienation—cosmic outcastness, developmental estrangements, historical loss, and self-estrangement—all of which, except for developmental estrangement, apply to this novel. See especially pp. 393–404.

50. *Red Harvest*, p. 57.

51. Ibid., p. 140.

52. Ibid., p. 142.

53. Ibid.

54. Ibid., pp. 166, 159.

55. Ibid., p. 186.

56. Hammett substantiates such a reading in his next novel, *The Dain Curse*, by having Mickey Linehan refer to the Op's responsibility for Dinah's death: "I ought to tell her what happened to that poor girl up in Poisonville that got so she thought she could trust you." *The Dain Curse*, p. 348.

57. *Red Harvest*, p. 185.

58. "Dreams and Genocide: The American Myth of Regeneration through Violence," *Journal of Popular Culture*, V. i. (Summer, 1971), 58.

59. Nolan, p. 7.

60. *Red Harvest*, p. 186.

61. Ibid., p. 187

62. "The Dashiell Hammett Tradition," p. 103.

63. "The American Detective Hero," *Journal of Popular Culture*, II 3 (1968), p. 400.

64. "Witness and Testament: Two Contemporary Classics," *Aspects of Narrative*, ed. J. Hillis Miller (New York: Columbia University Press, 1971), p. 174.

65. "The Night Is Dark and I Am Far from Home," *New American Review*, ed. Theodore Solotaroff (New York: New American Library, 1968), p. 90.

Chapter Four: *The Dain Curse*: A New Direction

1. Nolan, p. 51.

2. Ibid., p. 53.

3. "The Writer as Detective Hero," *The Mystery Writer's Art*, ed. Francis M. Nevins, Jr. (Bowling Green: Bowling Green University Popular Press, 1970), p. 303.

4. For a good discussion of the art of the traditional detective story, see Jacques Barzun, "Detection and The Literary Art," *The Mystery Writer's Art*, pp. 248–262.

5. William Kenney, "The Dashiell Hammett Tradition," p. 104.

NOTES

6. Barzun, p. 256.

7. Dashiell Hammett, *The Dain Curse*, p. 381.

8. Barzun, p. 253.

9. *Raymond Chandler Speaking*, ed. Dorothy Gardiner and Katherine S. Walker (Boston: Houghton Mifflin, 1962), p. 64.

10. See Kenney, p. 104.

11. *The Dain Curse*, p. 206.

12. Ibid., p. 207.

13. Ibid.

14. Ibid., pp. 248, 278, 330.

15. Ibid., p. 295.

16. Ibid., p. 306.

17. Ibid., p. 331.

18. Ibid., p. 345.

19. Barzun, p. 260.

20. "Introduction," *The Omnibus of Crime*, ed. Dorothy L. Sayers (Garden City and New York: Garden City Publishing, 1929), p. 33.

21. *The Dain Curse*, p. 330.

22. Ibid., p. 342.

23. Ibid., p. 344.

24. Herman Melville, *Moby Dick*, ed. Charles Feidelson, Jr. (Indianapolis and New York: Bobbs-Merrill, 1964), pp. 363–4.

25. Melville, p. 478.

26. *The Dain Curse*, p. 386.

27. Melville, p. 402.

28. See Nolan, p. 53. Replying to Philip Durham's charge that Hammett made the Op soft and old, Nolan argues that what he had in fact done was make him more "sensitive."

29. *The Dain Curse*, p. 386.

30. Ibid.

31. Ibid., p. 230.

32. Ibid., p. 245.

33. Ibid., p. 252.

34. Ibid., p. 287.

35. Ibid., p. 342.

36. Ibid., p. 348.

37. Ibid., pp. 248, 361.

38. Ibid., p. 356.

39. Ibid., p. 361.

40. Ibid.

41. Ibid., p. 373.

42. Ibid.

43. Ibid., p. 378.

44. Ibid., pp. 379, 384.

45. Ibid., p. 385.

46. Ibid., p. 379.

47. Ibid., p. 382.

48. Maurice Friedman, *Problematic Rebel: An Image of Modern Man* (Chicago and London: University of Chicago Press, 1970), p. 429.

49. See Elizabeth Sanderson, "Ex-Detective Hammett," *Bookman* 74 (January-February 1932), p. 518. Reprinted in Richard Layman, ed., *Discovering The Maltese Falcon and Sam Spade: The Evolution of Dashiell Hammett's Masterpiece, Including John Huston's Movie with Humphrey Bogart*, (San Francisco: Vince Emery Productions, 2005), pp. 68–70.

Chapter Five: *The Maltese Falcon*: The Emergence of the Hero

1. George J. Grella, "The Literature of the Thriller: A Critical Study." *Diss.* Kansas 1967, p. 53.

2. Robert I. Edenbaum, "The Poetics of the Private Eye: The Novels of Dashiell Hammett," *Tough Guy Writers*, p. 81. Reprinted in *The Critical Response to Dashiell Hammett*, p. 178.

3. Ibid., p. 81.

4. Ibid, p. 82. Unfortunately he never shows when Spade knows or how we know he knows. He may have his suspicions, but Hammett throws in enough red herrings to make certainty impossible.

5. Irving Malin, "Focus on *The Maltese Falcon*: The Metaphysical Falcon," *Tough Guy Writers*, p. 106. Reprinted in *The Critical Response to Dashiell Hammett*, p. 74.

6. Ibid.

7. Walter Blair, "Dashiell Hammett: Themes and Techniques," *Essays on American Literature in Honor of Jay B. Hubbell*, ed. Clarence Gohdes (Durham: Duke Univ. Press, 1967), p. 300. See also, Oscar Handlin, "Reader's Choice: Dashiell Hammett," *Atlantic Monthly* (July 1966), p. 137.

8. Ibid., p. 300.

9. Ibid., p. 306.

10. William P. Kenney, "The Dashiell Hammett Tradition," p. 111.

11. Letter to James Sandoe, January 26, 1944, Collected in *Raymond Chandler Speaking*, p. 48. Also in *Selected Letters of Raymond Chandler*, ed. Frank MacShane (New York: Dell, 1987), p. 26.

12. Edenbaum, p. 85.

13. Kenney, p. 110.

14. Ibid.

15. Ibid.

16. Ibid., p. 8.

17. Ibid., pp. 110–111.

18. Ibid., p. 110.

19. See George Grella, "Murder and the Mean Streets: The Hard-Boiled Detective Novel," *The Armchair Detective* (October 1971), p. 5. Originally published in *Contempora*, Vol. 1, No. 1, 1970. The proliferation of crime, Grella argues, is one of the usual themes in hardboiled detective fiction.

20. Dashiell Hammett, *The Maltese Falcon*, pp. 419–423.

21. Ibid., p. 433.

22. Ibid., p. 418. Italics are mine for emphasis.

23. Ibid., p. 425.

24. Edenbaum, p. 87.

25. *The Maltese Falcon*, p. 476.

26. See Grella, "Murder and the Mean Streets," p. 3. Grella argues that Spade is not concerned with moral questions, and to support his case points to the fact that he sleeps with his partner's wife, but this is not terribly convincing. One could just as easily point out that Spade shows a kind of morality by not continuing on in the affair once Brigid is on the scene. This might indicate that though he evidently had little respect for Archer, he had considerably more for Brigid.

27. *The Maltese Falcon*, p. 439.

28. Ibid.

29. Ibid.

30. Ibid., p. 445.

31. Malin, p. 107.

32. *Dashiell Hammett: A Casebook* (Santa Barbara: McNally and Loftin, 1969), p. 63.

33. *The Maltese Falcon*, pp. 442, 442–445.

34. Ibid., p. 445.

35. Kenney, p. 82.

36. Malin, p. 108.

37. Edenbaum, p. 83, 84.

38. *Hamlet*, V. ii, lines 166–170, pp. 344–345.

39. "A Cosmic View of the Private Eye," *Saturday Review* (August 22, 1953), p. 7.

40. Kenney, p. 108.

41. "Dashiell Hammett: Themes and Techniques," *Essays on Literature in Honor of Jay B. Hubbell*, p. 304.

42. Leonard Moss, "Hammett's Heroic Operative," *New Republic* (January 8, 1966), p. 32. Hostile to the detective genre in general, Leonard does not tell us why standards for evaluating individual rules within a genre must necessarily be "lenient."

43. *The Maltese Falcon*, p. 476.

44. "Dashiell Hammett's Microcosmos," *National Review* (September 20, 1966), p. 941.

45. *The Maltese Falcon*, p. 476.

46. Kenney, pp. 110–111.

47. *The Maltese Falcon*, p. 461.

48. See Malin, p. 107, for his discussion of Spade's "ceremonial" behavior; also, Edenbaum, p. 81, sees Spade as a man of no sentiment.

49. *The Maltese Falcon*, p. 461.

50. Ibid.

51. Ibid., p. 486.

52. Edenbaum, p. 85.

53. Ibid., p. 86.

54. *The Maltese Falcon*, p. 551.

55. Ibid., p. 553.

56. Edenbaum, p. 84.

57. See Harold Orel, "The American Detective Hero," *Journal of Popular Culture*, II.3. (1968), p. 399. Orel argues that "the seediness of Spade's surroundings is matched by a gray area in Spade's character: we are not always sure that he will reject a bribe, deny himself sexual indulgence, feel morally superior to the criminals he chases, or rejoice when he catches them. He is, indeed, remarkably like them," p. 399. Orel's description is accurate, but he fails to emphasize that this is how Spade wants to appear: it's all part of his role, and accounts for his success.

58. *The Maltese Falcon*, p. 551.

59. Ibid., p. 559.

60. Ibid.

61. Ibid.

62. See Edenbaum, p. 88. He says Spade knows all along that Brigid is Miles' murderer, an argument that cannot be proved by the text. In fact, in none of Hammett's novels do we know all the detective knows until the final chapters.

63. Kenney, p. 110.

64. Walter Blair, p. 110., does make such a claim, but Ben Ray Redman, "Decline and Fall of the Whodunit," *Saturday Review*, XXXV (May 31, 1952), pp. 8–9, ignores such a possibility , content with talking about sex in the novel only. Kenney, p. 95, says Spade "thinks he has fallen in love" with Brigid.

65. *The Maltese Falcon*, p. 521.

66. Edenbaum uses this piece of evidence as support for his point that Spade knows from the beginning that she is guilty. Hammett gives us no clue that this is so; just the opposite seems to be true, although we cannot be sure, positively.

67. *The Maltese Falcon*, p. 565.

68. "The Simple Art of Murder," *The Art of the Mystery Story*, ed. Howard Haycraft (New York: Simon and Schuster, 1946), p. 235.

69. *The Maltese Falcon*, p. 579. The italics are mine for emphasis.

70. Ibid.

71. Ibid., pp. 579–580.

72. Ibid., p. 582.

73. Ibid., pp. 580–581.

74. Ibid., p. 581.

75. Kenney, p. 99.

76. *The Maltese Falcon*, p. 581.

77. Ibid., p. 582.

78. Ibid.

79. See David Bazelon, "Dashiell Hammett's 'The Private Eye.': No Loyalty Beyond the Job," *Commentary*, VII (May 1949), p. 471. Reprinted in *The Critical Response to Dashiell Hammett*, p. 167. He says Spade finally chooses the job over sex.

80. Jean Paul Sartre, *Existentialism*, tr. Bernard Frechtman (New York: The Philosophical Library, 1947), p. 58.

81. *To Deny Our Nothingness: Contemporary Images of Man* (New York: Dell Publishing Co., Inc., 1967), p. 24.

82. *The Maltese Falcon*, p. 584.

83. Ibid., p. 583.

84. Edenbaum, p. 81.

85. *The Maltese Falcon*, p. 583.

86. In Hammett's early autobiographical short story "Holiday," the protagonist rejects a woman who strongly attracts him, resulting in "a warm feeling of renunciation flooding him. . ." See Hammett, *Lost Stories* (San Francisco: Vince Emery Productions, 2005), p. 115.

87. *The Maltese Falcon*, p. 584.

88. Paterson, "A Cosmic View of the Private Eye," p. 31.

89. Kenney, p. 113.

90. Paterson, p. 8.

91. Hammett, "Introduction," *The Maltese Falcon*. (New York: Modern Library, 1934), p. ix. Reprinted in *Discovering The Maltese Falcon and Sam Spade*, pp. 104–105.

92. Jo Hammett, *Dashiell Hammett: A Daughter Remembers*. (New York: Carroll & Graf, 2001), p. 32.

93. See Maurice Friedman, *To Deny Our Nothingness*, p. 245.

Chapter Six: *The Glass Key*: The Darkening Vision

1. Sanderson, "Ex-Detective Hammett," p. 518. Reprinted in *Discovering The Maltese Falcon and Sam Spade*, p. 70.

2. "Dashiell Hammett's 'The Private Eye': No Loyalty Beyond the Job," *Commentary*, VII (May, 1949), p. 471. Reprinted in *The Critical Response to Dashiell Hammett*, pp. 167–174.

3. "The Poetics of the Private Eye: The Novels of Dashiell Hammett," *Tough Guy Writers*, p. 99, 102, 100. Reprinted in *The Critical Response to Dashiell Hammett*, pp. 178–193.

4. "Decline and Fall of the Whodunit," *Saturday Review*, XXXV (May 31, 1952), p. 31.

5. "The *Black Mask* School," *Tough Guy Writers*, p. 70.

6. Durham, p. 70.

7. "The Simple Art of Murder," *The Art of the Mystery Story*, p. 236.

8. Charles A. Reich, *The Greening of America*. (New York: Random House, 1970), p. 44.

9. Letter to Bernice Baumgarten, April 21, 1949. *Raymond Chandler Speaking*, p. 56. Reprinted in *Selected Letters of Raymond Chandler*, p. 170.

10. "The Simple Art of Murder," p. 236.

11. "The Dashiell Hammett Tradition," p. 153.

12. Kenney. P. 111. Again we see Kenney's desire to see in Hammett traditional intentions and ideals.

13. Ibid., pp. 112–3.

14. Dashiell Hammett, *The Glass Key*, p. 598.

15. Ibid., p. 596.

16. Kenney, p. 96.

17. *The Glass Key*, p. 598.

18. Ibid., p. 771.

19. Ibid., pp. 636, 638.

20. Ibid., p. 683.

21. Ibid., p. 703.

22. It may be that Senator Henry's plea for a revolver is not motivated by a desire to commit suicide but a last ditch attempt to escape punishment by shooting Beaumont and even his own daughter. Hammett leaves it ambiguous, though I rather believe the former is true.

23. (New York: Random House, 1970), p. 30.

24. *The Glass Key*, pp. 775, 776.

25. Ibid., p. 776.

26. Ibid., pp. 776, 777.

27. Ibid., pp. 645.

28. Ibid., p. 648.

29. Ibid., p. 748.

30. D. H. Lawrence, *Studies in Classic American Literature* (New York: The Viking Press, 1966), p. 61.

31. See Charles T. Gregory, "The Pod Society Versus the Rugged Individualists," *The Journal of Popular Film*, I.1. (Winter, 1972), p. 11. Gregory's essay in part deals with the moral ambivalence of Don Siegel's detective movies, especially *Coogan's Bluff* and *Madigan*. A point he makes is that despite the almost inhuman violence of these heroes, their adherence to a personal definition of self and profession raises them above the "pod-like" conformists who are their colleagues.

32. "Dashiell Hammett's 'The Private Eye': No Loyalty Beyond the Job," p. 470.

33. Edenbaum, p. 100.

34. *The Glass Key*, p. 609.

35. Ibid., p. 676.

36. Hammett was a tuberculosis victim himself. He provides several indications that Ned Beaumont is tubercular. Several of these indications refer to Beaumont's thinness, a common symptom of the disease and the source of its then-popular name, "consumption": the comparison that Paul Madvig is "tall as Ned Beaumont, but forty pounds heavier without softness" (p. 592); Beaumont's "lean cheeks (p. 610); "Only the flatness of his chest hinted at any constitutional weakness." (p. 631, "constitutional weakness" being a euphemism for tuberculosis); and "tall and lean" (p. 654). Hammett also refers to Beaumont coughing, which is a symptom of tuberculosis (pp. 620, 627, and 741).

37. *The Glass Key*, pp. 611, 612.

38. Ibid., p. 687.

39. "Chandler and Hammett," *The London Magazine* (New Series), III, No. 12 (March, 1964), p. 78.

40. *The Glass Key*, p. 644.

41. Ibid., p. 652.

42. Ibid., p. 653.

43. Ibid., p. 672.

44. Ibid., p. 721: "He [Madvig] could have managed him [Taylor Henry] with one hand and he doesn't lose his head in a fight. I know that. I've seen Paul fight and I've fought with him."

45. Edenbaum, pp. 99–100.

46. Nolan, p. 70.

47. *The Glass Key*, p. 676.

48. Ibid., pp. 721, 723.

49. Ibid., p. 730.

50. Ibid., pp. 732–733.

51. Ibid., p. 736.

52. Ibid., p. 744.

53. Ibid.

54. Ibid., pp. 755–757.

55. Ibid., p. 745.

56. Ibid., pp. 761–762.

57. *An Unfinished Woman: A Memoir*, p. 225.

58. Edenbaum, p. 100.

59. *The Glass Key*, p 679.

60. See Ross-McLaren, "Chandler and Hammett," p. 78. He sees this as an indication that Beaumont may be falling in love with Janet, but I think that may be going a bit far. At best, it suggests Ned respects Janet.

61. *The Glass Key*, p. 746.

62. Ibid., p. 770.

63. Ibid., p. 774.

64. See Paterson, p. 31.

65. The Hamlet analogy again is useful here. Like Hamlet, Ned discovers that his world is not at all what he had imagined or hoped it would be.

66. Paterson, p. 8.

Chapter Seven: *The Thin Man:* The End Game

1. "Books," *New Statesman and Nation* (New Series), VII (May 26, 1934), p. 801. For a different view of Hemingway and Hammett see Joseph Haas, "Dashiell Hammett: Life 'by the Code,'" *Chicago Daily News*, June 18, 1966, "Panorama" section, page 7. Haas writes: "It seems probable that neither man was familiar with the works of the other, in those early years. What is likely is that their approaches were the products of two similar minds affected by comparable influence."

2. *Selected Letters of Dashiell Hammett*, p. 82.

3. Shaw, Joseph T. "Introduction," *The Hard-Boiled Omnibus: Early Stories from* Black Mask. (New York: Simon and Schuster, 1946), p. viii.

4. "Dashiell Hammett: Themes and Techniques," pp. 303–304.

5. "Donald E. Westlake Interview," bookreporter.com, 21 April 2000.

6. See "The Gangster Novel: The Urban Pastoral," *Tough Guy Writers*, pp. 186–198; "Murder and the Mean Streets: The Hardboiled Detective Novel," *Contempora*, I.1 1970, republished in *The Armchair Detective*, V.1 (October, 1971), pp. 1–10; "The Literature of the Thriller: A Critical Study." *Diss.* Kansas, 1967.

7. "Dashiell Hammett's 'The Private-Eye': No Loyalty Beyond the Job," p. 472.

8. "Decline and Fall of the Whodunit," p. 31.

9. Durham, "The *Black Mask* School," *Tough Guy Writers*, p. 71. The uncompleted first version of *The Thin Man* supports points made in this chapter. It is included in the Hammett anthologies *Nightmare Town*, ed. Kirby McCauley, Martin H. Greenberg, and Ed Gorman (New York: Alfred A. Knopf, 1999), pp. 347–396; and *Crime Stories and Other Writings*, ed. Steven Marcus (New York: Library of America, 2001), pp. 847–904.

10. "The Dashiell Hammett Tradition," pp. 106–7.

11. Kenney, p. 107.

12. Kenney, p. 106.

13. Kenney, p. 106. See also Wayne Booth, *The Rhetoric of Fiction* (Chicago and London: University of Chicago Press, 1961), p. 224. Booth shows why it is almost impossible to have dramatic irony and mystification simultaneously.

14. Kenney, pp. 86–7, 84.

15. "The Poetics of the Private-Eye: The Novels of Dashiell Hammett," *Tough Guy Writers*, p. 101.

16. Edenbaum, p. 102.

17. Keniston, *The Uncommitted* (New York: Dell, 1970), p. 391.

18. Kenney, pp. 86–7.

19. Kenney, p. 94.

20. Dashiell Hammett, *The Thin Man*, pp. 806, 809.

21. Ibid., p. 901.

22. Ibid., p. 790.

23. Ibid., p. 791.

24. See for example his decision to enter World War II at the age of forty-eight. Details can be found in William Nolan's *Dashiell Hammett: A Casebook* (Santa Barbara: McNally and Loftin, 1969), pp. 106–110. See also Jo Hammett, *Dashiell Hammett: A Daughter Remembers* (New York: Carroll & Graf, 2001), p. 116.

25. *The Thin Man*, p. 796.

26. Ibid., p. 806.

27. Ibid., p. 819.

28. Reported in Harold Orel, "The American Detective-Hero," *Journal of Popular Culture*, II. 3. (1968), p. 400.

29. "Cops, Robbers, Heroes and Anti-Heroes: The American Need to Create," *Journal of Popular Culture*, 1 (1967), p. 118.

30. "The Tough Hemingway and His Hard-Boiled Children," *Tough Guy Writers*, p. 21.

31. *The Thin Man*, p. 946.

32. "The Writer as Detective Hero," in *The Mystery Writer's Art*, p. 300.

33. Lillian Hellman, *An Unfinished Woman* (New York: Bantam Books, 1970), p. 167. Hammett and Hellman were living together while *The Thin Man* was being written. I have no doubt that Hellman influenced Hammett's handling of Nick and Nora. Recent research also shows that Hellman may have made an uncredited contribution to the writing of *The Thin Man*, just as Hammett acted as an uncredited contributor to some of Hellman's works, especially *The Children's Hour*, *The Little Foxes*, and *The Autumn Garden*.

34. See Kenney, pp. 83–4. He makes the excellent point that the corruption of the family unit suggests the larger corruption of society as a whole. Cf. George Grella, "Murder and the Mean Streets: The Hardboiled Detective Novel," *The Armchair Detective*, Oct. 1971, v. 5 n. 1, pp. 5–6.

35. Edenbaum, p. 102.

36. *The Thin Man*, p. 837. Hammett takes the Packer cannibalism story from Thomas S. Duke, *Celebrated Criminal Cases of America* (San Francisco: James H. Barry Co., 1910), pp. 309–310. Packer often spelled his first name as "Alferd," but Duke uses "Alfred," and Hammett follows Duke's spelling.

37. *The Thin Man*, pp. 787–788.

38. Ibid., pp. 807–808, 885, 898.

39. Ibid., p. 885.

40. Ibid., p. 812.

41. Ibid., pp. 916–917.

42. Ibid., p. 846.

43. In the 1934 first edition of *The Thin Man* published by Knopf and in the 1999 edition published by the Library of America, the character's name is Victor Rosewater. In *The Thin Man* included as part of *The Novels of Dashiell Hammett* (published by Knopf in October, 1965), the character is named Sidney Kelterman.

44. *The Thin Man*, p. 886.

45. Ibid., p. 924.

46. Ibid., p. 865.
47. Ibid., pp. 870, 871.
48. Ibid., p. 851.
49. Kenney, p. 87.
50. *The Uncommitted*, p. 49.
51. See George Grella, "Murder and the Mean Streets," p. 6. Speaking generally about Hammett, Chandler, and Macdonald, Grella makes the point that the hardboiled detective novel illustrates what happens when the "frontier" disappears and is replaced by the "urban jungle."
52. "The *Black Mask* School," *Tough Guy Writers*, p. 71.
53. See Walter Blair, pp. 304–5. See also note 43 above.
54. *The Thin Man*, p. 798.
55. Power of attorney: ibid., pp. 796, 821-822, 932, 938; money: ibid., p. 913.
56. Ibid., p. 937.
57. Ibid., p. 939.
58. Grella, "Murder and the Mean Streets," p. 5.
59. *Loss of the Self in Modern Literature and Art* (New York: Random House, 1962), p. 68.
60. Sypher, p. 66.
61. Summoning Camus here is not farfetched. See W. M. Frohocks, *The Novel of Violence in America* (Dallas: Southern Methodist Univ. Press, 1950), p. 13. We are told Camus imitated James M. Cain in *The Stranger*; Cf. Robert Edenbaum, p. 94. He compares the Hammett hero to Camus' man without a memory in *The Rebel*.
62. "An Imaginary Interview," tr. Malcolm Cowley, *New Republic*, CX (February 7. 1944), p. 186.
63. See Sypher's discussion of Heidegger's concept, p. 91 in *Loss of the Self in Modern Literature and Art*.
64. Frohocks, op. cit., p. 27.
65. *The Thin Man*, p. 941.

Chapter Eight: Conclusion: Form and Substance: An Overview

1. Quoted in L. E. Sissman, "Raymond Chandler Thirteen Years After," *New Yorker*, XLVIII (March 1972), p. 124.
2. L. E. Sissman, p. 124.
3. *The Dyer's Hand and Other Essays* (New York: Random House, Inc., 1962), p. 158.

Bibliography

Works by Dashiell Hammett

Dashiell Hammett Omnibus. New York: Grosset and Dunlap, 1930.

"The Need for Tempo in the Contemporary Novel" in *Fighting Words*, edited by Donald Ogden Stewart. New York: Harcourt, Brace, and Company, 1940, pp. 56–57.

Blood Money. Cleveland and New York: World Publishing, 1943.

Dashiell Hammett Mystery Omnibus. New York: World Publishing, 1944.

The Novels of Dashiell Hammett. New York: Alfred A. Knopf, 1965.

"The First Thin Man." *City of San Francisco*, 9, no. 17 (4 November 1975), pp. 1–12; reprinted in *Crime Stories and Other Writings*, below, pp. 847–904, and in *Nightmare Town*, below, pp. 347–396.

Complete Novels. New York: Library of America, 1999.

Nightmare Town, edited by Kirby McCauley, Martin H. Greenberg, and Ed Gorman. New York: Alfred A. Knopf, 1999.

Crime Stories and Other Writings, edited by Steven Marcus. New York: Library of America, 2001.

Selected Letters of Dashiell Hammett 1921–1960, edited by Richard Layman with Julie M. Rivett. Washington, D.C.: Counterpoint, 2001.

Lost Stories, edited by Vince Emery. San Francisco: Vince Emery Productions, 2005.

Works by Others

Angoff, Allan. "The World of the Detective Story," *American Writing Today*, edited by Angoff. New York: New York University Press, 1957.

Auden, W. H. "The Guilty Vicarage," in *The Dyer's Hand and Other Essays*. New York: Random House, Inc., 1962, pp. 146–158.

Barzun, Jacques. "Detection and the Literary Art," *The Mystery Writers Art*, edited by Francis M. Nevins, Jr. Bowling Green: Bowling Green University Popular Press, 1970, pp. 248–262.

Bazelon, David. "Dashiell Hammett's 'The Private Eye.': No Loyalty Beyond the Job," *Commentary*, 7 (May 1949), pp. 467–472; reprinted in *The Critical Response to Dashiell Hammett*, edited by Christopher Metress, pp. 167–174.

Bentley, Eric. "The Night Is Dark and I Am Far from Home," *New American Review*, edited by Theodore Solotaroff. New York: New American Library, 1968, p. 86–104.

Berthoff, Warner. "Witness and Testament: Two Contemporary Classics," *Aspects of Narrative*, edited by J. Hillis Miller. New York: Columbia University Press, 1971, p. 173–198.

Blair, Walter. "Dashiell Hammett: Themes and Techniques," *Essays on American Literature in Honor of Jay B. Hubbell*, edited by Clarence Gohdes (Durham: Duke University Press, 1967), p. 295–306.

Booth, Wayne. *The Rhetoric of Fiction*. Chicago and London: University of Chicago Press, 1961.

Boucher, Anthony. "There Was No Mystery in What the Crime Editor Was After," *New York Times Book Review*, 26 February 1961, pp. 4–5, 50.

Camus, Albert. *The Stranger*, translated by Stuart Gilbert. New York: Alfred A. Knopf, 1946.

———. *The Rebel: An Essay on Man in Revolt*, translated by Anthony Bower. New York: Alfred A. Knopf, 1956.

Carpenter, Frederic. "'The American Myth': Paradise (to Be) Regained," *PMLA*, 74 (1959), pp. 599–606.

Cawelti, John G. "The Spillane Phenomenon," *Journal of Popular Culture*, 3, no.1 (1969), pp. 9–22.

Chandler, Raymond. *Selected Letters of Raymond Chandler*, edited by Frank MacShane. New York: Dell, 1987.

———. *Raymond Chandler Speaking*, edited by Dorothy Gardiner and Katherine S. Walker. Boston: Houghton Mifflin Co., 1962.

———. "The Simple Art of Murder," *The Art of the Mystery Story*, edited by Howard Haycraft. New York: Simon and Schuster, 1946, pp. 222–237.

Connolly, Cyril. "The Private Eye: *The Raymond Chandler Omnibus*," Sunday *Times* (London), 23 July 1953.

Curti, Merle. "Dime Novels and the American Tradition," *Yale Review*, 26 (1937), pp. 761–778.

Daniel, Robert. "Poe's Detective God," *Furioso*, VI (1951), pp. 45–52.

Davis, David. *Homicide in American Fiction, 1798–1860: A Study in Social Values*. Ithaca: Cornell University Press, 1957.

Duke, Thomas S. *Celebrated Criminal Cases of America*. San Francisco: James H. Barry Co., 1910.

Durham, Philip. "The *Black Mask* School," in *Tough Guy Writers of the Thirties*, edited by David Madden. Carbondale: Southern Illinois University Press, 1968, pp. 51–79.

———. "The Cowboy and the Myth Makers," *Journal of Popular Culture*, (1967), pp. 58–62.

——. *Down These Mean Streets a Man Must Go: Raymond Chandler's Knight*. Chapel Hill: University of North Carolina Press, 1963.

——. "Hammett: Profiler of Hard-Boiled Yeggs," Los Angeles *Times*, 21 November 1965, Calendar section, pp. 1, 33.

——. "The Objective Treatment of the 'Hard-Boiled' Hero in American Fiction: A Study of the Frontier Background of Modern American Literature." *Diss.* Northwestern University, 1949.

——. "Riders on the Plains: American Westerns," *Neuphilologische Mitteilungen*, 58 (1957), pp. 22–38.

Edenbaum, Robert. "The Poetics of the Private-Eye: The Novels of Dashiell Hammett," in *Tough Guy Writers of the Thirties*, edited by David Madden. Carbondale: Southern Illinois University Press, 1968, pp. 80–103; reprinted in *The Critical Response to Dashiell Hammett*, edited by Christopher Metress, pp. 178–193.

Ellis-Fermor, Una. *The Jacobean Drama: An Interpretation*. New York: Alfred A. Knopf, 1964.

Fiedler, Leslie. *Love and Death in the American Novel*. New York: Criterion Books, Inc., 1960.

——. *No, in Thunder*. Boston: Beacon Press, 1960.

——. *Waiting for the End*. New York: Stein and Day, 1964.

Fishwick, Marshall. *The Hero, American Style*. New York: David McKay, 1969.

Friedman, Maurice. *Problematic Rebel: An Image of Modern Man*. Chicago and London: University of Chicago Press, 1970.

——. *To Deny Our Nothingness: Contemporary Images of Man* (New York: Dell Publishing Co., Inc., 1967.

Frohock, Wilbur Merrill. *The Novel of Violence in America*. Dallas: Southern Methodist University Press, 1950.

Frye, Northrop. *Anatomy of Criticism*. New York: Atheneum, 1966.

——. *A Natural Perspective: The Development of Shakespearean Comedy and Romance*. New York: Dell, 1967.

Fussell, Edwin. *Frontier American Literature and the American West.* Princeton: Princeton University Press, 1965.

Gardner, Frederick H. "Return of the Continental Op," *The Nation*, 203 (31 October 1966), pp. 454–456.

Gide, André. "An Imaginary Interview," translated by Malcolm Cowley, *New Republic*, 110 (7 February 1944), pp. 184–186.

Gores, Joe. "Dashiell Hammett" in *AZ Murder Goes Classic: Papers of the Conference.* Scottsdale: Poisoned Pen Press, 1997, p. 127.

Grebstein, Sheldon Norman. "The Tough Hemingway and His Hard-Boiled Children," in *Tough Guy Writers of the Thirties*, edited by David Madden. Carbondale: Southern Illinois University Press, 1968, p. 18–41.

Gregory, Charles T. "The Pod Society Versus the Rugged Individualists," *The Journal of Popular Film*, 1, no.1. (Winter 1972), pp. 3–14.

Grella, George. "The Literature of the Thriller: A Critical Study," *Dissertation*, Kansas 1967.

———. "The Gangster Novel: The Urban Pastoral," in *Tough Guy Writers of the Thirties*, edited by David Madden. Carbondale: Southern Illinois University Press, 1968, p. 186–198.

———. "Murder and the Mean Streets: The Hard-Boiled Detective Novel," *Contempora*, 1, no. 1, 1970; reprinted in *The Armchair Detective* 5, no.1 (October 1971), pp. 1–10.

Haas, Joseph. "Dashiell Hammett: Life 'by the Code,'" Chicago *Daily News*, June 18, 1966, "Panorama" section, page 7.

Hammett, Jo. *Dashiell Hammett: A Daughter Remembers.* New York: Carroll & Graf, 2001.

Handlin, Oscar. "Reader's Choice: Dashiell Hammett," *Atlantic Monthly* (July 1966), pp. 136–138.

Harper, Ralph. *The World of the Thriller.* Cleveland: Case Western Reserve University Press, 1969.

Haycraft, Howard, ed. *The Art of the Mystery Story.* New York: Simon and Schuster, 1946.

[223]

———. *Murder for Pleasure: The Life and Times of the Detective Story.* New York: Appleton-Century, 1941.

Hellman, Lillian. *An Unfinished Woman: A Memoir.* Boston: Little, Brown, 1969.

———. "Dashiell Hammett: A Memoir," *New York Review of Books,* 5 (25 November 1965), pp. 16–18, 20–23. Reprinted as "Introduction" to *The Big Knockover: Selected Stories and Short Novels by Dashiell Hammett.* New York: Random House, 1966. Also included as a chapter of *An Unfinished Woman, op cit.*

Jameson, Frederic. "On Raymond Chandler," *Southern Review,* VI (1972), pp. 624–650.

Jones, Archie. "Cops, Robbers, Heroes and Anti-Heroes: The American Need to Create," *Journal of Popular Culture,* 1 (1967), pp. 114–127.

Jones, Daryle. "Virgins, Villains, and Violence in the Dime Novel Western," *Journal of Popular Culture* 4, no. 2 (Fall 1970), pp. 507–517.

Keniston, Kenneth. *The Uncommitted: Alienated Youth in American Society.* New York: Dell, 1970.

Kenney, William. "The Dashiell Hammett Tradition and the Modern Detective Novel," *Diss.* Michigan 1964.

Klapp, Orrin. *Heroes, Villains, and Fools: The Changing American Character.* Englewood Cliffs, NJ: Prentice Hall, 1972.

Krutch, J. Wood. "Only a Detective Story," *The Nation,* 159 (22 November 1944), pp. 647–648, 652.

Lawrence, D. H. *Studies in Classic American Literature.* New York: Viking Press, 1966.

Layman, Richard, ed. *Discovering* The Maltese Falcon *and Sam Spade: The Evolution of Dashiell Hammett's Masterpiece, Including John Huston's Movie with Humphrey Bogart.* San Francisco: Vince Emery Productions, 2005.

Levin, Richard. "The Punitive Plot in Elizabethan Drama." *Diss.* Chicago, 1957.

BIBLIOGRAPHY

Lid, R. W. "Philip Marlowe Speaking," *Kansas Review*, 31 (1969), pp. 153–178.

Macdonald, Ross (Kenneth Millar). "Homage to Dashiell Hammett," *Mystery Writer's Annual*. New York: Mystery Writers of America, 1964, pp. 8, 24.

———. "The Writer as Detective Hero," *The Mystery Writers Art*, edited by Francis M. Nevins, Jr. Bowling Green: Bowling Green University Popular Press, 1970, pp. 295–305.

Madden, David. "James M. Cain: Twenty-Minute Egg of the Hard-Boiled School," *Journal of Popular Culture* I (1967), pp. 178–192.

———. ed. *Tough Guy Writers of the Thirties*. Carbondale, IL: Southern Illinois University Press, 1968.

Malin, Irving. "Focus on *The Maltese Falcon*: The Metaphysical Falcon," in *Tough Guy Writers of the Thirties*, edited by David Madden. Carbondale: Southern Illinois University Press, 1968, pp. 104–109; reprinted in *The Critical Response to Dashiell Hammett*, edited by Christopher Metress, pp. 74–78.

Massey, Irving. "Subject and Object in Romantic Fiction," *Symposium*, 11 (1957), pp. 185–203.

Maugham, Somerset. *The Vagrant Mood*. NY: Doubleday, 1953.

McLaughlin, Charles. "A Note on Imitation and Theme," *Journal of Aesthetics and Art Criticism*, 13 (1954–1955), pp. 268–269.

Melville, Herman. *Moby Dick*, ed. Charles Feidelson, Jr. Indianapolis: Bobbs-Merrill, 1964.

Metress, Christopher, ed. *The Critical Response to Dashiell Hammett*. Westport, CT/London: Greenwood, 1994.

Michael, M. Scott. "The Hard-Boiled Detective Novel," *The Writer*, 57 (March 1944), pp. 105–107.

Moldenhauer, Joseph. "Murder as a Fine Art," *PMLA*, 83 (1968), pp. 284–297.

[225]

Mooney, J. M. "The American Detective Story: A Study in Popular Fiction." *Diss.*, Minnesota, 1968.

Moss, Leonard. "Hammett's Heroic Operative." *New Republic*, 154 (8 January 1966), pp. 32–34.

Murch, A. E. *The Development of the Detective Novel*. Port Washington: Kennikat Press, 1968.

Nolan, William F. *Dashiell Hammett: A Casebook*, Santa Barbara: McNally and Loftin, 1969.

Orel, Harold. "The American Detective Hero," *Journal of Popular Culture*, 2, no.3 (1968), pp. 395–403.

Ornstein, Robert. *The Moral Vision of Jacobean Tragedy*. Madison: The University of Wisconsin Press, 1960.

Parkes, Henry. "Metamorphoses of Leatherstocking," *Literature in America*, edited by Philip Roth. New York: Meridian Books, 1957, pp. 431–445.

Paterson, John. "A Cosmic View of the Private Eye," *Saturday Review* (22 August 1953), pp. 7–8, 31–33.

Phelps, Donald. "Dashiell Hammett's Microcosmos," *National Review* (September 20, 1966), pp. 941–942.

Queen, Ellery (Frederic Dannay and Manfred B. Lee). *In the Queen's Parlor*. New York: Simon and Schuster, 1957.

———. *Queen's Quorum*. New York: Little Brown, 1951.

Quennel, Peter. "*The Thin Man*," *New Statesman and Nation* (New Series), 7 (May 26, 1934), p. 801.

Redman, Ben Ray. "Decline and Fall of the Whodunit," *Saturday Review*, 35 (May 31, 1952), pp. 8–9, 31–32.

Reich, Charles A. *The Greening of America*. New York: Random House, 1970.

Rolo, Charles J. "Simenon and Spillane: The Metaphysics of Murder for the Millions," *New World Writing*. New York: New American Library, 1952, pp. 234–245.

Ross-McLaren, J. "Chandler and Hammett," *The London Magazine* (New Series), 3, no. 12 (March, 1964), p. 78.

Sanderson, Elizabeth. "Ex-Detective Hammett," *Bookman* 74 (January-February 1932), pp. 516–518; reprinted in *Discovering The Maltese Falcon and Sam Spade* edited by Richard Layman, pp. 68–70.

Sandoe, James. *The Hardboiled Dick: A Personal Check-List*. Chicago: Arthur Lovell, 1952; reprinted in *The Armchair Detective*, 1, no. 2 (January 1968), pp. 38–42,

Sartre, Jean Paul. *Existentialism*, translated by Bernard Frechtman. New York: The Philosophical Library, 1947.

Sayers, Dorothy L. "Introduction," *The Omnibus of Crime*, edited by Dorothy L. Sayers. Garden City and New York: Garden City Publishing, 1929, p. 33.

———. *Unpopular Opinions*. New York: Harcourt Brace, 1947.

Seelye, John. "Buckskin and Ballistics: William Leggett and the American Detective," *Journal of Popular Culture* I (1967), pp. 52–56.

Shakespeare, William. *The Tragedy of Hamlet*, edited by G. R. Hibbard. Oxford: Oxford University Press, 1987.

Shaw, Joseph T. "Introduction," *The Hard-Boiled Omnibus: Early Stories from* Black Mask, edited by Shaw. New York: Simon and Schuster, 1946, pp. v-ix.

Shaw, Peter. "The Tough Guy Intellectual," *Critical Quarterly* 8, no.1 (Spring 1966), pp. 13–28.

Shied, Wilfrid. "The Good Word: It All Depends on Your Genre," *New York Times Book Review* (5 September 1971), pp. 2, 22.

Sington, Derek. "Raymond Chandler on Crime and Punishment," *Twentieth Century*, CLXV (1959), pp. 502–504.

Sissman, L. E. "Raymond Chandler Thirteen Years After," *New Yorker*, 48 (March 1972), pp. 123–125.

Slotkin, Richard. "Dreams and Genocide: The American Myth of Regeneration through Violence," *Journal of Popular Culture*, 5, no. 1. (Summer 1971), pp. 38–59.

Smith, James W. "The Indestructible Hero," *Commonweal* 67 (1958), pp. 147–149.

Symons, Julian. *The Thirties: A Dream Revolved.* London: Cresset Press, 1960.

Sypher, Wylie. *Loss of the Self in Modern Literature and Art.* New York: Random House, 1962.

Thompson, Alan R. "The Cult of Cruelty," *Bookman* 74 (January—February 1932), pp. 477–487.

Willett, Ralph. "The American Western: Myth and Anti-Myth," *Journal of Popular Culture* 4, no. 2 (Fall 1970), pp. 455–463.

Wilson, Colin. *The Outsider.* New York: Dell, 1965.

Wilson, Edmund. "Who Cares Who Killed Roger Ackroyd?" *New Yorker* 20, no. 49 (20 January 1945), pp. 52–58.

———. "Why Do People Read Detective Stories?" *New Yorker* 20, no. 35 (14 October 1944), pp. 78–84.

Winthrop, Henry. "Pop Art as an Expression of Decadence," *Journal of Popular Culture* 2, no. 2 (1968), pp. 228–239.

Index

[229]

U

V

W

Y

About the Contributors

Writing a doctoral dissertation on Dashiell Hammett led **GEORGE J. "RHINO" THOMPSON, PH.D.,** to change his career from university English teacher to police officer. He became the author of the bestseller *Verbal Judo: The Gentle Art of Persuasion* and the founder and president of the Verbal Judo Institute. "Rhino" has been featured on network news on NBC, ABC, CBS, CNN, and Fox, and on the TV programs *48 Hours, Inside Edition,* and *In the Line of Duty.* He lives in upstate New York. His website is www.verbaljudo.com.

WILLIAM F. NOLAN is a two-time winner of the Mystery Writers of America's Edgar Award. In addition to writing three nonfiction books about Dashiell Hammett, Nolan is the author or co-author of thirteen novels, including the multi-million seller *Logan's Run,* and many screenplays and biographies.

VINCE EMERY edited *Lost Stories* by Dashiell Hammett and has contributed research and articles to several books about Hammett. He also wrote the bestseller *How to Grow Your Business on the Internet.*

Title page artist **LEE WALTER GRUBAUGH** (1920-1988) graduated from the Yale University School of Art, served in the U.S. Air Force during World War II, and worked as a commercial and fine artist, and as a designer of commemorative coins. His painting "The Gateway to the West" hangs in the White House.

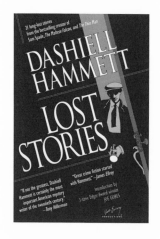

21 long-lost stories by the creator of Sam Spade, *The Maltese Falcon*, and *The Thin Man*

- Featured Alternate Selection, The Book-of-the-Month Club.

- Featured Alternate Selection, Mystery Guild.

- Selected by *The Wall Street Journal* as one of 10 books recommended as Christmas gifts for mystery fans.

- Selected by Thrilling Detective.com as one of 9 books recommended as Christmas gifts for private eye fans.

- "Pierce's Pick of the Week," *January Magazine*.

Otto Penzler, *New York Sun*: "A hugely important book. It belongs on the shelf of every detective fiction reader and collector. It is a book to be read with pleasure."

Michael Rogers, *Library Journal*: (Starred review) "Lost might be an overstatement, but these 21 Hammett mysteries are tough to find elsewhere, and it's great having them together. Hammett's *Lost Stories* is must reading for mystery buffs."

Connie Fletcher, *Booklist*: (Starred review) "These 21, long-out-of-print stories find Hammett at or near the top of his game, his signature hard-boiled style shining brightly."

Peter Handel, *Pages:* "A marvelous collection of previously unpublished works by the ever intriguing Pinkerton detective-turned-writer. What makes the compilation a cut above the usual is Emery's annotations to each story, placing it in a specific context of Hammett's life at the time of writing. Great fun, but historically important, too."

Dashiell Hammett, the bestselling creator of Sam Spade, *The Maltese Falcon,* and *The Thin Man,* was one of the America's most entertaining authors, and one of its most influential. Even so, many of Hammett's stories—including some of his best—have been out of the reach of anyone but a handful of scholars and collectors—until now.

Lost Stories rescues 21 long-lost Hammett stories, all either never published in an anthology or unavailable for decades. For each story, Hammett researcher Vince Emery tells how Hammett's life shaped the story and how the story affected his life. To round out this celebration of Hammett, three-time Edgar Award winner Joe Gores has written an introduction describing how Hammett influenced literature, movies, television, and Gores' own life.

Edited by Vince Emery. 8 illustrations, 38 photos; 352 pgs.

Trade hardcover edition: $24.95. ISBN 0-9725898-1-3. Available from booksellers everywhere.

Deluxe collector's edition: Limited to 195 hand-numbered copies, each signed by Joe Gores and Vince Emery. Housed in a decorative clothbound slipcase with color front and back art panels. Spine of Saderra leather and front cover of book are stamped with genuine gold. Page edges are gilt. Printed on archival-quality paper. Decorative colored endpapers. $149.95. Available at www.emerybooks.com.

The evolution of Dashiell Hammett's masterpiece, including John Huston's movie with Humphrey Bogart

- Edgar Award nominee, Best Critical/Biographical Book of the Year

- Selected by the *Los Angeles Times* as one of 10 recommended gifts for movie buffs.

- Selected by *The Wall Street Journal* as one of 10 books recommended as Christmas gifts for mystery fans.

- Selected by Thrilling Detective.com as one of 9 books recommended as Christmas gifts for private eye fans.

Kenneth Turan, *Los Angeles Times*: "A treasure beyond price for fans of both the classic Hammett novel and the three (that's right, three) film versions of the doomed quest for a black bird. An incredible amalgam of photos, memos, letters, reviews, whatever, this will make fans of the book or the film gasp as one unexpected delight succeeds another. With this book, wonders really do never cease."

Michael Rogers, *Library Journal*: (Starred review) "This one-stop resource is a … dream. Highly recommended."

Tom Nolan, *Los Angeles Times*: "Amply and inventively illustrated, [it] holds a wealth of source material. There are too many other highlights in this marvelous reference work to list, let alone describe. [The novel and films are] superbly documented and appreciated by this unsurpassed reference tribute."

Gary Lovisi, *Hardboiled:* "A glorious celebration of the tough private eye and the greatest hard-boiled book ever written."

Kevin Burton Smith, Thrillingdetective.com: "The perfect gift for fans of Sam Spade, Hammett, film noir, and the history of cinema and literature."

Dashiell Hammett's novel *The Maltese Falcon* is often named as one of the twentieth century's best novels. John Huston's film adaptation is one of the first examples of film noir. It made Humphrey Bogart a star, and was selected by the American Film Institute as one of the 100 greatest movies of all time.

Now, *Discovering The Maltese Falcon and Sam Spade* uncovers from institutional and private archives a wealth of treasures about Hammett's masterpiece, his detective Sam Spade, the three film versions of the novel, stage adaptations, Sam Spade short stories, radio shows, and even comics. Many of the discoveries here are previously unpublished. The book provides hundreds of rare documents and original source materials, including production notes for the three movie versions.

Contributors include Dashiell Hammett himself, plus Jo Hammett, Richard Layman, Mary Astor, Joseph Shaw, Dorothy Parker, John Huston, Hal Wallis, Darryl F. Zanuck, Joe Gores, William F. Nolan, and more than fifty additional writers. It is illustrated with more than 200 photos, illustrations, and facsimiles. The book is a joy for fans of Hammett, Sam Spade, detective fiction, film noir, and the history of literature and cinema.

Paperback edition, $19.95. ISBN 0-9725898-

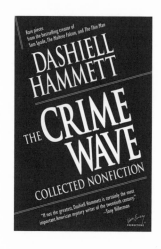

The Crime Wave: Collected Nonfiction by Dashiell Hammett

Dashiell Hammett is famous for his fiction, but he also wrote nonfiction: book reviews, magazine articles, and more. *The Crime Wave* is the only collection of Hammett's nonfiction.

The Crime Wave includes Hammett's suggestions on how to write well, his views on good mysteries and bad ones, his political writings, his techniques for creating effective advertisements, his history of the World War II Battle of the Aleutians, and the complete text of all of his newspaper columns, "The Crime Wave."

Most of the rarities in *The Crime Wave* have never been available in book form. Editor Vince Emery provides introductions and notes to put each selection in context. For readers interested in Hammett, in detective fiction, or in twentieth-century American history and culture, *The Crime Wave* provides source material and insights available nowhere else.

Deluxe collector's edition: limited to 150 copies, $149.95. Available from www.emerybooks.com. ISBN 0-9725898-4-8X

Trade hardcover edition: $24.95. Available in 2007 from bookstores everywhere. ISBN 0-9725898-5-6